Searching for...
LIGHT in the Darkness

Danney Clark

To Saleena
with best wishes

Dan Clark

DanScribe
Publishing

DEDICATION

Dedicated to all who follow Jesus even when it is difficult
and those who work tirelessly to achieve and advance
God's kingdom here on earth.

ACKNOWLEDGEMENTS

To God, our Creator, author and finisher of our faith,
to friends, fans, and family who
provide encouragement and inspiration
and my friend and editor Larry Patrick who works
tirelessly to get each book into print,
thank you.

Many want to treat God like small children who are eager to help Mom out in the kitchen. They accommodate them by allowing them to scramble the eggs but push back when it comes to frying the bacon which might pop and burn them.

It is not until you can trust God that you will see that His mercy and love are large enough to do everything that is necessary and more.

~ Danney Clark

Table of Contents

Cremains

Cremains: A term used for the human remains following cremation, ash. Regardless of the cause of death, the method of disposition of the body is the final question to be answered here on earth, however, not so for the soul of the newly departed.

He was devoid of true human emotion, it was as though from birth he had been controlled by the evil that so plainly now had manifested itself in him. He killed without regret, with flair and flourish, enjoying each gritty detail as would a rapist enjoy memories of his sordid conquests. But now time was drawing near for his capture, the net was tightening around him; the thousands of hours of investigation by local police and now the FBI were beginning to find traction. Somehow they had gotten a DNA sample, and somehow it had been traced back to him. It was but a matter of time before he slipped up and they took him.

The darkened street was poorly lit by the scattered streetlights in the aged neighborhood, they gave him just enough light to make his way silently along without being noticed. The houses were mostly square boxes with pitched roofs and wide front porches across their breadth, sided with narrow wood and most painted light colors, with a darker contrasting trim. The sidewalks running across the spacious front lawns were sunken and heaved by the roots of the great trees that lined the narrow street. The neighborhood had a look of permanence and stability about it, but underneath the façade, when observed more closely, age and decay caused by years of neglect were easily apparent.

A few of the homes were dimly lighted, each by a single porch light that failed to illuminate the fenced-in front yards or the sidewalk beyond. He felt satisfaction in knowing his prey was unaware of his presence and if noticed, he could easily pass himself off as a visitor who had lost his way. Nothing about him warned of the evil in his heart, to the contrary, he looked if anything too ordinary, too non-descript for anyone take notice.

Thirty-nine by his count, and he was meticulous in keeping accurate count of his victims, had fallen to his lust for murder. Still he was not satiated, he craved even more blood and more obscene and painful forms of torture and death at his hand. He liked the older neighborhoods where new age families moved, trying to capture a rural America of which they had never been a part.

The twenty and thirty something's looking to live in Mayberry, USA, while feeling safe and secure, in harmony with nature. He loved the fact they'd drive miles in their new Subarus and spend a hundred dollars to buy a plastic container to accumulate their recyclables so they could blame others for wasting resources.

A stooped, aging man with a dog on a short leash was approaching him, his head down, watching his footing on the uneven cement. First the mutt, he thought and then the old codger, but quickly dismissed the idea as being too easy. As they approached, the old dog gave a throaty growl before being quieted by his master who then passed without looking up. Should listen to your dog you old fool, he thought to himself, he knows danger when he smells it.

At the corner he turned right, not because he had a destination in mind, but because he could avoid crossing the street and possibly be noticed by a passing car while under the street light. His mind was always active, he had a natural intuition for such things he often reminded himself, a gift, if you will. He laughed to himself, not a God given gift for sure, but a gift all the same. Alleys, the older neighborhoods always had alleys, where stray dogs overturned trash cans looking for a meal and cats in heat made their sorrowful plea for satisfaction. Easy entrance, easy exit was his mantra... use what you have and make the best of it.

He was not a large man, but fit and strong, maniacally strong when adrenaline coursed through his veins as he sprang into action. A dusting of grey at the temples gave him what he thought was a 'mature' look that belied his age. At thirty-five, he looked nothing like the picture on his photo ID unless one looked closely at the relationship of his eyes and nose. Most would have taken him for mid to late forties. He liked to fanaticize that he was an agent for some covert government operation or a gun for hire catering to the rich and famous. In truth he was neither, he was simply a deranged and sadistic murderer with a certain talent and a passion for his hobby.

Claude Dallas, the name appealed to him, so he adopted it as his own. In reality he had heard the name of the self-confessed mountain man who had killed and then hidden the bodies of two law enforcement men in the Idaho wilderness. Somehow the murders had been justified by an unknown survival code left over from centuries past. The original Dallas had done far less time in prison because of that "old west" mindset of the jurors. Educated and articulate, this Claude Dallas prowled the streets of the cities rather than the sagebrush covered wastelands of Idaho, but he too justified his need to kill.

~ ~

"You have been found guilty by a jury of your peers," the judge announced sternly, "for the murders of nine innocent human beings. Do you have anything to say before I pronounce sentence?"

Brent T. Williams/Dallas was standing beside his court appointed attorney when the verdict was announced. He smiled sardonically, looked hard into the eyes of each juror then back at the judge, but said nothing. The courtroom was silent except the whispered comments from the gallery.

Again the gavel called the assembly to attention before the judge continued. "Having been found guilty for nine counts of the crime of premeditated murder in the first degree you are hereby sentenced to death by hanging, sentence to be carried out thirty days from today."

Other jurisdictions had taken a backseat rather than pursuing their own murder charges with the hope that justice would be executed swiftly here, thus saving them the time and costs of separate trials.

As the court was adjourned, Dallas was led from the room in shackles and taken to his cell. Outside of the courthouse, a large crowd had assembled including newsies and the families of the many victims who hadn't fit within the confines of the courtroom. Since his reign of terror had spanned seven states and involved more than a dozen communities, the national as well as local press abounded. The deferred sentencing of thirty days was the standard time to allow counsel to appeal the verdict, which he did not.

~ ~

Fresh red blood overflowed his swollen and torn lips and ran freely down his chin, then fell onto his chest. His white t-shirt was sodden and stained crimson all down its front. A pitiful moan, almost like the mewing of a cat, issued from him as if his soul had given itself over to despair. Behind him, on an ancient table covered with litter and years of accumulated dirt, sat a new cordless variable speed drill. It, like its owner, was splattered with blood and tissue but neither seemed to care.

"I've always wanted to do a root canal," Dallas said to himself as much as his victim, "and now you have given me that opportunity, thank you."

Securely held in the drill chuck was a long slender drill bit measuring $1/8$" inch in diameter. It, of course, had been the instrument which Dallas had applied to several healthy teeth of the man securely zip tied to the sturdy metal office chair sitting before him. The victim seemed to find renewed energy as he strained in vain against his restraints. The nylon ties cut deeply into his flesh, causing blood to flow freely from them. He seemed to neither notice nor care that he was further injuring himself, he was desperate to escape or die in the process, now knowing that his assailant had not one speck of mercy in his black soul.

"Please, please rest yourself," Dallas said with mock sincerity. "You'll need that energy before our night together is finished."

Paul, the young collegian who had stopped and attempted to help an injured motorist, cried silently, praying as he did. His only chance, he knew, was if someone noticed his car and called the police to investigate. But, he knew that even if they did, there was nothing to indicate where he had gone or that he had not simply walked away from the car. Nothing at the scene indicated foul play or that someone should find cause for worry before morning. By morning, he knew he was certain to be dead.

"You cut my hand you know," Dallas stated in a monotone voice, "you shouldn't have done that. Your struggle proved to be futile as you now can see, so why cause me pain unnecessarily?"

Paul would have smiled if his swollen lips would have allowed. So he thought, he had given his captor a small amount of pain in return.

Just knowing that he had bled and that he would carry even a small scar pleased the young man. He attempted dialogue but without success as his mouth failed to form words.

As he looked, he could easily see the hand in question, it was dressed and taped as though by a professional but showed a crimson stain against the whiteness of the gauze. His eyes roamed the expanse of the room where he sat bound and hidden from view. It appeared to be some sort of shed or barn he reasoned, on some long abandoned farm not far from where his captor had staged the accident scene.

Dallas seemed preoccupied with rearranging the meager contents of the confinement. The table, though roughly built and unfinished looked sturdy, much like some kind of workbench. He cleared it, carefully setting aside the drill and the few articles he had brought with him in the black nylon gym bag, which sat on the floor nearby. He made a grand gesture of sweeping its dusty surface with a ancient broom that had made itself available.

His eyes swept the room, taking note of articles that had been left behind by their former owner, first stopping on a rusty metal baled hay hook with its point buried in a low hanging rafter, then a pitchfork with a broken handle that leaned against an outside wall. Paul shuddered involuntarily as he too took notice of them.

~ ~

"Keys are still in it," the young State police officer stated as he walked cautiously around the perimeter of Paul's Subaru, "looks like someone from the university by the parking sticker and the books in the back seat."

He kept his flashlight trained on the car while carefully approaching the driver's door. His backup stood to the rear and left of the rear fender, his hand on his weapon, eyes sweeping the area.

"Wait," he said, alarm registering in his voice, "there's blood, blood on the steering wheel. Keep me covered while I open the door."

Overhead, the moon was playing hide and seek behind the low scattered clouds, giving the scene an otherworldly feel. One might almost expect that a zombie may find his way out of the ditch and make his way onto the roadway, dragging a foot behind him.

The cruiser behind Paul's car was parked at a slight angle with its lights flashing, indicating the need for caution and to protect the officers from injury from an errant rubber-necker. The senior officer, the one who still stood behind the car, made a call to the station using his shoulder mounted radio. He described the scene in detail and asked for a second unit.

When that second unit came, it was Detective Jamison and his partner Maria Cortez, both seasoned investigators and both assigned to the "Monster Man" murders, as the press called them. They had been chasing the suspect from county to county for months and were in constant communication with FBI profilers and law enforcement in six other states.

The vehicle, abandoned without apparent cause, was one of the commonalities in nine of the thirty-nine known slayings, but this one was different, here there was blood evidence to collect. The others had yielded nothing until the dismembered corpses had been found weeks later.

Cortez opened the driver's door gingerly with her gloved hands, half expecting that something would leap out... nothing did. Inside, a quick appraisal confirmed the trooper's initial opinion. A student from the local university had met with foul play. She carefully broke the seal on a forensic swab and took a liberal sample of the blood residue still drying on the steering wheel and followed it up with many pictures from several angles, including the photo ID of Paul Billings that was hanging from the rear view mirror. Those she immediately transmitted to the station via her smart phone. The blood samples were rushed to the lab for analysis by the second team who arrived after Cortez.

Jamison walked up and asked, "anything besides the blood peak your interest?"

"I find it strange that there is significant blood on the wheel but none in the seat or carpet," Cortez answered. "If the boy just cut himself why didn't he just wrap something around it and keep driving?"

Jamison nodded. "And if he was badly hurt, why is there no body?"

"Over here," one of the patrolmen said, shining his flashlight on the ground, "more blood."

Between the cars, nearly obscured by the rough surface of the asphalt, were three significant pools of blood rapidly drying and turning brown.

Jamison shook his head, then said, "We'd better give the whole area a good look, the boy may have wandered off the road into the brush and be bleeding to death."

The four split up, two on each side of the roadway, moving slowly into the brush and then looping a hundred yards above and below the vehicles. They found nothing, nothing at all, no sign of blood or other human activity.

"If he was bleeding that badly, we'd have found something," Jamison said to his partner. She nodded her agreement.

"Maybe he caught a ride," Cortez offered, "maybe we should put a call out to the local hospitals."

It was Jamison's turn to nod, "good thinking," he said smiling, "you'll make a detective yet."

Cortez was already on her radio with the station, alerting them to the possibility that the boy needed medical attention, several minutes later she was interrupted by a call from the forensic department.

"The blood type is A negative, it is not from our missing student. I have confirmed from his medical records that he is O positive."

"Hear that?" Cortez said, turning to Jamison, "the blood on the wheel is from an unknown and not our missing college boy."

Hope blossomed within them, both hoping that they finally had a concrete lead.

~ ~

"Well, my young friend, we have been blessed with a sturdy work table and vintage instruments left behind for our use," he said to Paul.

Paul did not give him the satisfaction of knowing the fear that gripped his heart, and also did not speak out, possibly fearing he'd speed up the process that his captor had in mind.

A sturdy wooden handle made to be gripped in the hand with a long heavy metal hook protruding from it had found its way onto the table. In years past, a pair of them would have given a strapping farm worker an easy grip when handling baled hay.

Dallas had found a ladder and was intently focused on moving a rusty pulley that was hanging from a rafter to re-attach it above the table. A substantial rope trailed from either side of it, easily reaching the floor on both ends. Paul tried to focus on anything and everything around him to keep his mind off the pain in his mouth and the fear that caused his sweat to turn cold on his skin.

"I'm thinking you'll be late for class on the 'morrow," Dallas said humorously, attempting to engage his victim in conversation without luck. "I fear you may have wasted the whole semester," he added.

Paul held his tongue, which had swollen in his mouth, making it difficult to breathe, forcing him to abstain from any attempt at conversation.

"You'll have the distinction of being number forty," Dallas said to the dusty barn, uncaring if the boy replied or not. "That's quite a feat, if I do say so myself, and not a single clue left behind."

"What about the blood?" Paul mumbled through swollen lips. "Do you think they will not notice the blood?"

He was hit in the head by the metal hay hook for his trouble, which Dallas had taken care to use the side rather than the point. Blood streamed from the cut where the skin had parted on his crushed eye socket.

"So what if they do?" Dallas said, his voice full of fury. "You'll pay dearly for cutting me!"

Paul had closed the door on his assailant's hand, nearly severing his little finger, before Dallas had dragged him from the car and disabled him with a syringe. He was proud that come what may, the monster would carry scars to his grave. He winced as he watched Dallas deftly tying a noose in one end of the old farm rope.

~   ~

Jamison was on the phone with the FBI agent, talking in hushed tones, when Cortez approached their car. Why he had lowered his voice she failed to understand, no one was within five miles of the place except the two patrolmen. Maybe just force of habit, having spent years in the bullpen at the station where everyone listened to everything about everyone. Where nothing was private and the more you tried to make it so, the sharper the ears listening in.

"Vic #12 had her breast nearly bitten off," Jamison reminded his partner. "Fibbi has a DNA sample from the saliva to compare with our blood sample, betcha lunch that they match."

"You are on," Cortez answered. "This is one I hope I lose. When will we know?"

"They're on it now," the senior detective answered. "Within the hour is my guess. They're sending a chopper with a team out to give the area a once over tonight rather than waiting until morning."

Cortez smiled. Jamison noted that when she smiled she became beautiful, not just good looking, but beautiful. She had just enough Latin blood to give her color but not enough to cause you to envision her short and squat in their old age like many of her ancestors. He had to admit he was attracted to her but knew well that they could never be a couple.

~ ~

Dallas sat in his cell pondering the events that had led to his capture and cursing himself for leaving the woman's body intact enough to get DNA samples. He should have burned her, he thought; his vanity had been his undoing. He had left the body in plain sight out of spite, just daring the authorities to figure him out.

Nineteen days remained before the execution, nineteen days to remember and enjoy each of the thirty-nine once again. It was like sex to him. He could relive the past and enjoy it anytime he chose.

He did not fear death, he had seldom even considered or worried about it. He had always lived in the present and for the day. Now his days were numbered and although he tried to dismiss it, apprehension crept into his conscious thought more frequently now.

Questions came, taunting him, questions about the eternal nature of man, questions about what happened when his eyes would close a final time. As a child he'd had few friends, he'd preferred to be alone and spurned the attempts of others to draw him into their foolish games. His father, if one could call him that, was seldom at home and when he was, he seemed to take particular pleasure in beating his wife and children. He had come home from the service a broken man who sought release from his demons in a bottle.

Dallas learned early on that when the sound of the old pickup approached the house, he should make himself scarce. As a teen he'd catch stray cats and enjoy their ritual torture and killing, each seemed to wear the face of his father.

One evening, just before his sixteenth birthday, his father had caught him in the old garage behind the house indulging himself with a girlie magazine he'd stolen from the market. He crept up behind him and hit him hard with his fist. Dallas fell unconscious into the firewood stacked against the wall. The old man sat down on a bench with the magazine and a bottle and drank himself to sleep.

When Dallas awakened, cut and bleeding, his father was still passed out. He'd poured lawn mower gasoline over the sleeping form, dropped a match and closed the door as he left.

~   ~

Back in the barn once again, Dallas took a syringe and plunged it into Paul. Almost immediately he could feel the warmth spreading throughout his body, his thought process became fuzzy, his limbs heavy, then he was unconscious. Dallas cut the zip ties that bound him to the chair and slipped the noose over his head and downward over his shoulders and under his arms, then snugged it up around his chest.

As the rope drew taught, Dallas could see his victim was struggling to breathe. He did not hesitate but took pleasure as the struggling form was hoisted up, then lowered onto the waiting work table. The noose was loosened, then moved again upward until it was once more around the sleeping man's neck.

Dallas stripped the helpless man of his clothes, then secured his naked body to the sturdy legs of the table with lengths of rope, leaving the slackened noose around his neck. Power, it was all about power Dallas thought, about having the power of life and death – he felt like God standing in this deserted barn deliberating the fate of his latest victim.

As he thought back over the various types of abuse he'd heaped upon his previous victims, it occurred to him that the actual death itself held little value, the path taken which precipitated it aroused him and brought the pleasure. He'd make sure this buff young specimen lived to see the coming dawn.

~ ~

The chopper had landed on the highway just a few minutes before, disgorging a half dozen darkly clothed figures from it. They spread out in a military fashion, searching meticulously the same area the two troopers and detectives had an hour before. Three more figures exited behind them and walked directly to the patrol car where Jamison and Cortez sat drinking coffee from their thermos.

"We covered that," Jamison offered, motioning to the brushy area beside the road.

The lead agent, sporting a bullet proof vest across her large chest, ignored him. She obviously wasn't used to sharing command with locals. The two detectives left the warm vehicle and walked to where the Fibbies stood a few feet away.

The agent, a rather tall and efficient looking woman, inclined her head slightly and announced, "Special Agent Bode." She was flanked by a tall black man and a Caucasian, both of whom could well have passed for NFL linebackers.

"Smith and Jones," she added, jerking her finger over her shoulder. Had the scene been different, the two detectives would surely have laughed at what seemed to come right out of "Men in Black."

"Detectives Jamison and Cortez," Bill Jamison said politely. "We've been expecting you. Have you brought news with you about the DNA sample?"

Cortez thought, how like her partner to cut right to the chase, unimpressed with the woman or her entourage. As a matter of fact, she liked everything about him and suspected he had similar feelings for her. They had spent many nights together on stakeouts, following up leads, and investigating clues, but never had they enjoyed physical intimacy. It would ruin it, she thought to herself, like a television series where the viewer can tell when the writers are running out of material and finally let the heroes bed each other.

"Agent Bode" it seemed, wasn't used to answering questions from what she figured were her subordinates, but she acquiesced to Jamison's persistent manner. "Yes, we have a positive match on a sample from a previous killing," she answered, without elaborating.

"Vic #12, who had been molested and partially eaten," Cortez asked, getting into the fray. "Kathleen Simmons of Riverdale?"

She was rewarded with a nod, before Special Agent Bode spoke. "We have reason to believe that this victim may still be in the surrounding area. We intend to do a pre-dawn search with the helicopter."

"Are you familiar with the area?" Jamison interceded. "There's a lot of country around here where someone could hide, abandon buildings and old farm houses."

A look of frustration was apparent in the FBI agent's face, but just as quickly it softened and her tone changed to that of honey, much like a school girl needing a favor. "Well, Detective Jamison," she purred, "I was hoping I could rely on you to provide that."

Jamison unfolded a county map across the hood of their cruiser as they gathered eagerly around and began pointing out areas he felt may be suspect. In less than a minute it was clear that they needed him aboard the craft, directing their search.

"We've only room for eight," Bode said apologetically, looking Cortez straight in the eye, "perhaps you could chauffeur some of my ground crew while I coordinate the search from the air."

Cortez smiled, holding her teeth together a bit longer than necessary, and then answered, "that alright with you, Jamison?"

"Couldn't think of anyone more capable, or anyone who knows the area as well," he answered. "Why don't you take Smith and Jones with you and let them get a feel for our little county?"

He added, "Seriously, Lupe, do me a favor and wear the vest this time."

In the four years they had ridden together he had never used her first name, never. She had wondered if he had even known it until now.

~ ~

"Oh, there you are, back from your little nap," Dallas exclaimed as Paul opened his eyes. At first he had trouble focusing, and then trouble recognizing the view of the rafters which now were above him. He strained futilely against the tethers that held him to the table.

"I've been thinking," Dallas said, as though visiting with a friend, "about how we should end this." He continued, "would you care to weigh in on how you'd like to spend your last few hours?"

Paul was tempted to say, 'just get it over with, make it quick', but then he realized it would never be so. Just the opposite, his captor enjoyed the game, and relished the pain each felt before going into eternity, so he held his tongue.

Dallas walked to a support timber near the head of the table, loosed the end of the rope from it, and as he did, he applied downward pressure, tightening the noose around Paul's neck and lifting his head.

Fear immediately filled Paul's eyes and he was rewarded with a smile from Dallas.

"No, not now at least," he said. "Maybe later, after we've gotten to know each other a little better." Dallas let the rope slacken in his hands.

Paul wondered if anyone had noticed that he had not returned to his dorm room, and if they had, would they take time to care? Most would just assume he'd worked late or was at the library studying for mid-terms. Unlike many, he was a Christian and not part of the social scene where partying went unbridled day and night. Had he been, no one would have missed him for weeks, if ever. He prayed asking for God's solution to this unspeakable nightmare that he was living. No answer came, no hint even that anyone heard.

"Are you cold?" came an unusual question from Dallas. "I could find something to cover you," he volunteered.

How odd, Paul thought, that in the midst of all this his tormentor would be worried if he was cold. But the savage laugh that followed assured him that the offer had been a lark, meant only to amuse the man.

~ ~

Jamison, Bode, and the remaining six who had searched the area boarded the helicopter. As the pilot brought up the RPM's, Bode turned on the overhead map light and spread the map out on the small table between them. Jamison had given a duplicate to Cortez after having circled and labeled the search quadrants with corresponding numbers.

"Where do we start?" Bode asked, nearly shouting as the big bird lifted from the ground.

Jamison pointed to the adjacent field to their left, then back at the map to an area circled and labeled #1. "We might as well start at the beginning and work our way outward," he answered with a smile.

As the helo gained altitude, the pilot turned on the infrared scanners and immediately received over a hundred heat signatures for his trouble. Bode leaned forward in the seat and tuned the sensitivity which eliminated all small animals and reduced the number by 90%.

First they flew the perimeter of the quad noting homes with sleeping forms lying side by side, small herds of animals, probably deer moving through the brush, and a handful of individuals seeming to ignore the fact that it was 3:00 a.m., moving about inside their homes. Most Jamison knew well, some by name and others by location, none raised suspicion.

On the ground, Cortez had done as Jamison had asked, taken and strapped on her bulletproof vest. Her companions must have been born in theirs and grown into them, she concluded, or possibly they had been specially tailored to fit their massive physiques.

The conversation between the chopper and the patrol car was minimal until a questionable barn, shack, or house needed the personal touch. Lupe would wind down each long rutted drive with lights out and personally inspect each, with her two goons by her side.

~   ~

The cell was cold and dark, only an occasional sound from one of the other inmates gave indication that the structure was inhabited. Dallas lay on his back, eyes open, staring into the impenetrable darkness, his mind bursting with questions without answers. He had not shut his eyes in 48 hours, not for a moment, not wanting to waste a single second of the time left to him.

Of course he could not stay awake for the fifteen days that remained before his sentence was to be carried out, it was not physically possible. He had tired of reliving the death of his victims several days ago and seemed to lack other stimuli to keep his mind active. He tried reading, exercise, even meditation, but nothing worked.

"What if" questions bombarded his brain... what if this... what if that... questions without seeming relevance or answers.

Maybe it will be better this way he said to himself, maybe the pain in my heart will stop when my heart stops. He had always felt incomplete, and except for those brief times when hate or lust filled him with power, he always felt empty and lost, almost childlike.

How, he questioned, had he been able to function among them without notice, for forty years? No one seemed to notice, no one seemed to care. He'd never had a close friend, male or female, never enjoyed consensual sex, never a shared kiss. He'd not expected anyone to understand; indeed, he did not understand himself why he was so different.

~ ~

Eight of the twelve quads had been carefully flown over and investigated, without a hint of a suspect. It was a little after four when Jamison looked down on the old Baker place from several hundred feet above and noticed a gray sedan parked near the barn. The farmhouse had fallen to ruin several years before under the weight of the winter snow, but the massive barn had fared far better, leaning only slightly on its foundations.

"Cortez, this is Jamison," he said, stating the obvious. "We're out at the old Baker place, got two heat sigs inside the barn, one vehicle outside. It has cooled down enough not to register on the scanner, must have been parked here for several hours."

"Roger that," Cortez affirmed, "we're about three miles out, headed your way."

"There's a light on inside," Jamison added. "Must be a portable. There has been no power to the place in years."

"10-4," Cortez said automatically. "We can be there in ten minutes."

"Whoa, slow it down Lupe," Jamison said earnestly. "We are going to land in the clearing near the beaver pond about a mile from your 20, we'll walk in together."

The adrenaline was pumping now, each of them could feel the burst of energy it carried with it, and each eager to see who occupied the old barn. Jamison tried to tell himself it was probably vagrants or lost travelers holding up for the night, but his instincts said better. Bode made contact with control and apprised them of the situation and their pending plan.

~   ~

Dallas had been humming to himself as he prepared to open Paul's heart cavity with a scalpel he'd purchased at the thrift store. It had been his dream since he was a child to hold a beating human heart in his hand, as he had done with the neighbor's cat. He stopped humming, listened intently after thinking he'd heard something overhead in the darkness. The sound did not repeat itself so he concluded it was a bird or bat trapped high in the rafters, beating its wings.

"Now this may hurt a bit at first when I break the skin," Dallas apologized to his captive patient, then hesitated and added, "but as soon as I get through the dermis and start cutting muscle and bone, it's going to hurt like hell." He laughed at his own joke.

"I suppose there's little reason to use antiseptic or take precautions to keep this sanitary," he said more to himself than Paul, "you won't live long enough after the surgery to get an infection."

Paul felt a sense of calm come over him, his fear and panic seemed to dissolve into the night air. He felt the presence of Jesus in the room and knew then that nothing or no one had control over the scene except his Savior. He closed his eyes and prayed, his ears refused to hear the mad ramblings of his captor.

Interestingly he prayed not for release but for peace and strength, eventually he prayed for Dallas as well. Time seemed to be standing still. When he opened his eyes, Dallas had not moved, nor had he began his lurid attempt at heart surgery.

~   ~

It had always been easy for Dallas to make the connection with the evil that lurked in his heart. He just opened up to it and it would come and fill him. But now, somehow it was different, even the memories of his tainted past would not return for him to enjoy and savor once again. Something powerful seemed to be standing between him and the rage and hate that had been his life. When he entreated the evil one to join him in the cell, nothing happened.

Outside the morning's light was just dawning signifying the beginning of a new day and putting an end to the one just past. To Dallas, it signified the beginning of the final week of his life. He'd had little to do, sitting alone in his cell with only an hour a day to walk the exercise yard, but to count the minutes and hours and days until his execution. It had been three weeks since the sentence had been imposed in a courtroom full of press and onlookers.

As he had been led from the courtroom by his jailers, he had noticed Paul in his peripheral vision, sitting by himself, his head bowed. They did not make eye contact or exchange words. During the trial, when Paul had been called to testify, he had seemed reluctant to do so. Even though his testimony was the most damning and probably made the prosecutions case air-tight, he had only answered the questions asked. without interjecting emotion or personal comment.

"You have a visitor," the jailer announced. "Back up against the bars with your hands behind you."

With practiced efficiency, handcuffs were secured around his wrists before the cell door was unlocked.

~ ~

They gathered beside Cortez' cruiser in the darkness, speaking in hushed tones, in spite of the fact that the barn was still nearly two miles down the rutted dirt road. Instinctively, each chambered a round and lowered the hammer of their weapons before setting their safeties. In turn, each checked the fit of their vests, tightening a Velcro fastening here and there to afford maximum protection. Jamison smiled at the sight of his partner in her vest.

Bode, of course, resumed command, both of her own agents and included the two detectives in her orders. "When we have the barn in sight, we'll break up into three groups and come at it from three sides, leaving one clear in the event we need to fire our weapons. Smith and Jones will each lead one and I and the two detectives the third. Is that clear?"

All heads nodded and mumbled an affirmative answer. The nine of them took to the road at a brisk pace, trying to watch their footing as they did. Beside the road, willows and brush had encroached many places, making it necessary to move in single file. Night sounds filled the stillness of the summer air and an occasional movement nearby from some wild animal caused them to halt and hold their collective breaths.

About fifteen minutes later the brush and trees opened into a cleared farm field, some quarter of a mile across and twice as deep. The ruins of a turn-of-the-century farmhouse lay in a heap a hundred or so feet from the massive barn. Several ghostlike pieces of abandoned farm equipment rose above the tall pasture grass like soldiers at arms. Only a very faint glimmer of subdued light shone through the cracks in the barn door. As the air stirred and blew toward them, Cortez thought she heard a muffled voice, but was not sure.

Bode lifted her hand and made a fist, the group froze in response, then fell in behind their leaders and moved toward their objective, slowly and quietly. Jamison took the right side, Cortez the left, while Bode set the pace in the center. Stopping just before the three groups lost sight of each other around the corners of the structure, she held up five fingers indicating five minutes to breach, then moved to the barn door while her command approached from opposite sides.

Much like the movies, where the police burst into the room with great noise and yelling, they burst into the sanctity of the barn, weapons raised. Beside the single lantern on a makeshift operating table, the naked form of a young man lay tied and immobile. Beside him, with a raised hand holding a scalpel, was his would-be killer.

With a certain dignity and an amused smile, he laid the instrument beside his victim and said, "so it was your transportation I heard overhead and not some errant barn owl after all."

~ ~

Sitting quietly at a table in the visiting area, a Bible open before him, sat Paul Billings. Paul raised his head when the door opened, then stood while two large deputies and the shackled prisoner, he had known only as Dallas, emerged. Dallas' hands had now been cuffed in front of him and were quickly attached to a metal ring in the table, which was secured to the concrete floor. One of the uniformed guards bent and whispered instructions to Paul before moving away.

The two men, now in reversed roles, eyed each other before speaking. Dallas tried to assume control, putting on a false bravado when he said, "and what brings you to my humble home, are you here to gloat?"

"No, Mr. Williams," Paul said quietly but firmly. "I am here to speak with you privately about an issue of deep concern to me, your eternal life."

Dallas/Williams paled but said nothing.

"In a very short time now you'll be stepping from this life on earth into a new one which will last forever," Paul stated. "Are you aware of that?"

Paul waited while Dallas seemed to absorb what had just been said.

"I thought you were a college student, not some preacher," Dallas answered, avoiding the question, but sounding far less in control of his emotions.

Paul just waited, saying nothing.

Dallas tried again. "You some Watchtower or something, come to convert me? You are a little too late for that."

"It is not about me, what I can do, or even what I want," Paul replied quietly.

"I saw you praying as you laid there on the table, praying for God to save you from my knife. Must have worked, here you are, and here I am," Dallas said with conviction.

"I wasn't praying just for myself," Paul said. "I was praying for you too, praying that God would give you one more chance."

Dallas felt a foreign emotion... regret. He had never felt regret before, or compassion, or anything at all beyond his personal wants and needs.

"I'm beyond salvation, too little, too late," Dallas said. "Even if there is a God, I've made too many bad choices."

"Is there a devil?" Paul asked, "Is there evil in the world?"

Dallas nodded.

"Then if the devil is real, there is a hell." He continued, "it figures then that there is also a God and a heaven. Can you believe that?"

Again Dallas agreed, but without speaking.

Paul lifted the Bible he had been reading from the table, holding it above his head, "and this is the Word of God. Every word in it is true because God cannot lie and God says that none are beyond His power to save." He opened the book to Romans and slowly read Romans 3:28 and Romans 6:23, pausing often to let the impact of the words enter into the man across the table from him.

"No one, none are beyond redemption and those who repent of their sins and choose to accept Jesus' gift of salvation and declare it before God and man are saved and will live forever with Him in heaven."

Something was definitely going on in Dallas' heart, something like he'd never felt before. The Holy Spirit was speaking to him, reassuring him, taking away his pain, doubts, and fears... Paul could sense it. "Tell me, Mr. Williams, do you believe what I am saying is true?"

The room was quiet; several of the others in the room had stopped their meaningless chatter and were listening intently to the conversation. There were none present that did not know of the "monster murderer" sitting with them or had heard the horror stories of his legacy.

Dallas was holding his breath, afraid to speak, fearful of the emotions that were overwhelming him. He was near to tears and frightened to show it. His arrogant posture changed, his shoulders dropped, and his head lowered in submission to the King. "Yes, yes," he finally said quietly, "forgive me," and then, raising both his head and voice, said again, "Forgive me Lord Jesus for all that I have done."

The End

Dementia

Prologue

For those of you who have read others of the author's works and wondered why he hasn't been institutionalized, I am afraid this new offering will do little to comfort you or answer the question. Please enjoy the diversity that the author offers within this book's cover.

~ ~

He died in her arms, his muscles quietly relaxing, the struggle for life ended, a smile rapidly disappearing from his lips. She opened her mouth to wail but no sound issued from her lips; grief consumed her, swallowing her up like the sea would swallow a small boat. Her mind felt almost vacant, disbelieving that what she knew to be true could really be happening. They had been married less than six hours, and yet their life together was over almost before it began....

She was fourteen when she first saw him and his family moving into the old Claiborne house just down the street. The U-Haul was backed into the driveway with a trailer on behind. From the first she knew they'd fit well into their poor, aging neighborhood. Their old sedan looked a dozen or more years old and the battered pickup filled with junk furniture parked at the curb, was still older yet.

She sat innocuously on her front porch swing and watched as they made trip after trip from first the trailer and then the cube van and into the house. There looked to be three or possibly four in the family. From where she sat she couldn't be sure because their faces were often hidden by the armloads of boxes and household furnishings they carried. When her mother joined her on the swing, Cassie called her attention to the new residents. Her mother nearly leaped from her seat, speaking over her shoulder as the old screen door slammed behind her. "I need to get something in the oven, something to take over to welcome them."

Cassie felt a little uncomfortable and ashamed that she had sat watching for a half hour and had not considered that at all. She knew she'd been raised better, she told herself she should have at least gone over and offered to help them. She pulled on her tennis shoes but left the laces loose the way she liked them, rather than tying them up tight, checked the window as she walked by to make sure she was presentable, and walked down the steps to the sidewalk before turning toward the Claiborne's. Of course it was not theirs anymore, she reminded herself, not since she had died and he'd gone to live with his children.

It was the end of the summer of 1967, the Beatles, Monkees, and The Who were taking the United Kingdom by storm, and with their eyes on America and the world. Cassie had turned fourteen in July and began her journey to womanhood. Viet Nam had been an undeclared war for a dozen years, with casualties mounting and spoiling the revelry that the anti-war hippie movement enjoyed. Free love was to become "free everything" generations later, as the nation turned to one of entitlement rather than hard work.

She had just reached the driveway as he came running around the side of the van and collided with her, knocking them both to the lawn, dazed and confused. She could feel the bump on her head swelling even before she came to grips with what had happened. A thin trickle of blood spilled down his chin from the tear in his bottom lip which also had begun to swell. Too old to cry, they both forced themselves to laugh.

"Are you alright?" he asked first, offering her a hand after he got to his feet.

"Yeah, I think so," Cassie answered, and then added, "but I think I'm turning into a unicorn."

That brought a painful laugh to his split lip, followed by an "ouch."

"You're new," she said, stating the obvious for lack of something more noteworthy to say.

"No," he answered. "I'm fourteen, haven't been new for a while."

"I mean, you are new to the neighborhood," she corrected, "my name is Cassie Newell." She stuck out her hand like she was greeting someone at church.

He was smiling crookedly, obviously his lip was causing him some pain, when he answered, "pleased to meet you Cassie Newell, I'm Joel Rasmussen, pronounced like Noel from the Christmas carols."

They both laughed self-consciously before she asked, "may I help you unpack?"

Before he could answer his father yelled, "Jo-ell, where are you, I need a hand with this dresser."

"Comin' Dad," he yelled as he headed back around the van, with Cassie at his heels.

Joel's dad was standing at the back of the trailer, one end of a large dresser lifted waist high, looking for someone to take the other. He was tall and spare, well over six feet, with disproportionately long arms and a skinny neck with a protruding Adam's apple. Cassie would have laughed as Ichibod Crane came immediately to mind but resisted the urge.

"Dad," Joel said quickly, "this is Cassie, she has come to help us unload."

"Great," he said with a grin, "grab on."

Not waiting to see if he was kidding or not, Cassie grabbed the free end of the dresser and hefted it off the ground while Joel stood with his mouth open.

"I'll follow you," she said, trying to sound confident that she really could.

They made it to the back bedroom and sat the dresser down just before she would have had to ask for a break.

"Bill," Joel's father said, extending his hand with a look of respect in his eyes. "I'm pleased to meet you Cassie."

That was the beginning of a friendship that would transcend life's mortal boundaries.

~   ~

It happened that Bill was the new basketball coach at the high school and taught American History to the freshman class. Quite by coincidence, both Joel and Cassie were in his third period class. Cassie had wondered if their blossoming friendships may cause a problem, they did not. Joel and Cassie both treated Bill with the respect due a teacher and few even were aware that Bill was Joel's dad until later in the school year. He in return, treated them as students, without giving them any special recognition or accommodation.

The family had moved from Lancaster to take the vacant position as head basketball coach and teacher. Mrs. Rasmussen was a homemaker and peacemaker. A devout Christian woman, she jumped right into service at the local church, with the youth group and also volunteered her services with the choir. 'Stout' was a term that best described her, physically, emotionally, and spiritually. God had given her the gift of inner strength and a dash of vitality that kept her in constant motion.

While Bill put in long hours teaching, coaching, and grading papers in his home office, his wife gradually turned the Claiborne house into the Rasmussen home. The yard once again was filled with color as new plantings grew and blossomed, the old garden spot in the backyard was cleared, tilled, and was waiting for the spring to allow it to produce its bounty. Bill could be seen on weekends with Pam at his heels, trimming and pruning, as she pointed out errant limbs and branches.

The Rasmussen's also had a daughter, Mary, who had been given to them late in life and who was born with both physical and mental disabilities. She could speak but chose not to most of the time. More often than not she could be seen in her wheelchair out in the yard, dressed warmly, keeping her mother company as Pam, with hard work and determination, gradually turned it into a showplace. Like so many, Cassie had little experience with the disabled and felt uncomfortable and ill at ease around Mary. But soon Mary's winning smile and light blue eyes melted her heart and drew her into the younger girl's world.

It was Down's syndrome, she'd been told, before taking the time to research and understand it better, which had caused her unusual look and mannerisms. Cassie's first life lesson was to allow God to change her and recreate her heart until she could love as He loves. She grew to love Mary as the sister she'd always wanted.

~ ~

They were interrupted by the sound of the doorbell ringing. Outside on the step, standing in the open doorway, was Cassie's mother Beth with a smile and freshly baked rolls. In her other hand was a pot roast with vegetables. She was welcomed in and introduced around before the threesome left the two women and Mary to visit and continued their quest to unload the waiting furniture.

It was weeks later before Bill and Al, Cassie's father, met one morning while mowing their front lawns. This time it was Bill who made the walk down the street to introduce himself to his new neighbor.

"Bill," he said as Al shut off his mower and moved toward the outstretched hand.

"Al," came the response as they automatically assessed one another.

"Cassie has told us a lot about you," Al remarked. "Said you are coaching the varsity team this fall. Are they going to be any good?"

"They ARE good," Bill answered. "My job is to help them become better."

Al nodded, then asked, "you fish?"

"Love it, when I can find the time," Bill replied, smiling.

"Maybe you and your son can join Cassie and me some time and take the boat out," Al offered. "Since Cassie has grown up it gets harder and harder to get her to come along," he added.

Bill looked a little doubtful. "Fall's the best time for hunting and fishing and is also the busiest for a coach getting ready for the season ahead."

Al looked a little deflated so Bill added, knowing that to reject the gift is to reject the giver, "maybe I could schedule a late practice on a Saturday and go up with you in the morning. Is there a good place close?"

Al regained his usual smile, "nice reservoir twenty minutes from our driveway, the Kokanee fishing in the spring and fall is great, that's when you find them schooled up."

"Cow bells and Ford fenders, leaded line?" Bill exclaimed excitedly.

"Right on the money," Al affirmed. "With a wedding band and night crawler on behind them."

The two men acted as though they'd been friends for years... such is the way of fishermen.

While the men schemed and planned their trips to the lake, Beth and Pam also were becoming close friends. They attended the same Bible study group, worked together in their yards, shared downtime with each other while enjoying afternoon visits and as always, Mary was nearby.

Cassie had always been a good student, making her grades with what seemed little effort or study. Joel on the other hand, did not live in the abstract but had a 'show me' mind that wanted to see and feel, not theorize and dream. That mindset served him well in sports activities where he could practice and see what was expected, but less well in solving mathematical equations. They spent an increasing amount of time studying together as he worked to keep his scholastic eligibility to play sports. Cassie admired the almost carefree way he seemed to approach life, while he looked with awe at her disciplined study habits and ability to understand the theoretical.

It had just been a look, but unlike any of the thousands before it, their eyes locked and their hearts touched for the first time. Unknown to all but themselves, they had made an unspoken commitment to each other that first moment when they realized they shared something wonderful. Embarrassed, they both had been quick to try and joke it away, but it stayed and grew and filled each up with a longing for a lifetime to spend together. Neither had known love except as that of a family member, neither had hereto felt the tingle in their stomachs which represented a longing to share themselves exclusively.

By the summer of their sophomore year, Joel had both a car and a full time job, working after school and on weekends. They shared quality time but little of it as he hustled to bank money for college which was but a few scant semesters away. Rather than count on an athletic scholarship and find himself disappointed, he wanted to have at least the first year's tuition in the bank. Cassie liked his approach to covering his bases, to her it showed the maturity that a woman would want in a husband. Although they had not yet even kissed, their hearts seemed to be making plans for the future.

~   ~

Al and Bill were inseparable, bowling on Tuesday nights, watching sports together on television, and fishing and duck hunting as occasions presented themselves. Neither of the men however, seemed to have a desire to do more than escort their families to church on Sundays, then to come home to football. Beth and Pam often spoke about how they wished their husbands were more spiritual and occasionally tried to push them toward a commitment. It did not work.

Like so many moral men with a good sense of right and wrong, neither considered themselves the targets of the Pastor's sermons which spoke of sin and sinners. They judged themselves incorrectly as good people, better than most, and not in need of Jesus' sacrifice.

The team was in the playoffs with smart money betting on them to take the state championship when Bill's star forward was caught cheating to stay eligible. He'd been paying others to do his homework and had been caught with a crib sheet in use during the semester test. The eyes of the school, as well as parents at home, were on the new coach to see how he would handle it. When Bill walked out of the principal's office where he, the student, and his parents had spent two hours, he was red faced and angry.

Going in he had determined that the young man would have to pay for his conduct by sitting out the rest of the season, but the principal and the parents had argued for forgiveness and not suspension. He'd lost his battle when the father had asked, "have you never lied or cheated, are you perfect?"

The team was eliminated in the first round when it could not regroup and keep politics off the court. Some argued for and others against their teammate, in the end the divided were conquered. When Bill came home after the game he poured himself a drink and sat down to brood. Beth's attempts to comfort him made him all the more angry and distant. They had their first angry argument, which ended with her leaving in tears.

She and Pam went to the church library where it was quiet to talk, while Bill invited Al over to listen as he unburdened himself. Meanwhile, Joel and Carissa tried hard to understand the double standard that was applied to the situation, each having an opinion and making valid points about justice and forgiveness.

Later in the week, Pastor Donovan listened to the two women and answered their questions with a question of his own. "Why does God not allow man to judge himself?"

Both gave a great deal of thought before they each answered. Donovan disregarded their attempts and answered quietly, "man is not qualified because he is imperfect, he'll either error on the side of justice and persecute the repentant, or on the side of mercy forgiving the unrepentant one. Only God knows the heart."

~ ~

Out of pride Bill had seriously considered resigning, his family however finally prevailed, pleading that they had too much invested in their home and community to leave and move on without a job. Bill secretly worried how his defeat would affect his career as a coach. With their season effectively over, he maintained a low profile hoping that the problem would go away, but it did not. Both students and teachers seemed to be taking sides on the issue regardless of the fact they had no investment in the controversy.

About a week after the season ended, his assistant coach asked to meet with him on a Saturday for lunch. Bill mentally braced himself for the encounter, expecting either a resignation or a useless show of support too long after the fact. Tim was a young man, ten years Bill's junior, with a young pretty wife and one small child. He guessed him to be only a half dozen years out of college. When he entered the sandwich shop he was immediately disarmed by the broad smile and pleasant greeting of his assistant.

"Thank you for meeting me, Bill," he began. "I know you are busy both at school and at home, but I thought we should visit."

Bill began to return the pleasantries but was cut off.

"I've been watching you since you arrived, and have learned a lot from your steady hand on the tiller," he said. "I admire you and your ability to teach and grow young men."

Again Bill attempted to interrupt unsuccessfully.

"But," (isn't there always a but, Bill thought to himself). Tim continued, "it seems that you have come to a place in life where you need more than you have to give."

Bill was immediately angry and was ready to say so when the younger man held up one hand and said, "please let me finish."

"Are you a Christian?" he asked Bill point blank, stopping his angry retort mid-stride and causing him to refocus and think.

"Yes, of course I am," Bill began while resenting Tim's inflection. "I go to church, what difference does that make about anything?"

"It makes all the difference," Tim answered.

"Are you saying I was wrong?" Bill thundered.

"I'm saying that no matter which side you chose you were doomed to fail, because God was not in the decision," the young coach answered firmly. "It is called 'operating in your own wisdom' by we who believe."

Bill was not ready yet to listen, he was still angry and resented being spoken to this way by his subordinate. "So, you are saying I'm not a Christian and that I don't listen to God?" he said in a raised voice.

One had to give Tim credit for staying cool under pressure. "What I am saying is that I'm not sure that you know what being a Christian is. Being a Christian is not a name but a way of living."

Finally Bill felt defeated and tired, with no desire to continue to argue and it showed in his demeanor.

"Lunch is ready," Tim said jovially while jumping to his feet and retrieving their sandwiches, "what do you want to drink?"

Just like that, the discussion changed and Bill felt more at peace than he had in a long time. "Coke I guess," he answered, feeling a need to help Tim, but also not having the energy to do so.

Tim returned with a tray and a smile, "my treat, Coach," he said before bowing his head.

Bill did likewise and listened as the young man asked God's blessings on the meal and their time together.

They ate in silence for a few minutes before Bill spoke, "Tell me about yourself," he asked.

Tim seemed pleased to have been asked and started right from the beginning, describing his childhood, his family, his upbringing, his mediocre talent in various sports, his choice of colleges and his conversion to Christianity while still in grade school. As he relived his testimony he seemed to grow in stature and wisdom, Bill thought. He ended by telling of his chance meeting with his wife Amy and of their new child Tasha. He sat back eating and said, "your turn."

Bill felt kind of bland and uninteresting as he tried to imitate Tim's description of his short walk through life. The only high spots were the births of his two children and... of course his marriage to Pam. He was thinking of how poorly he'd look to others if they were reading the obit which gave his life's accomplishments.

Tim just sat there listening, then said, "and......?"

"And what?" Bill responded, a little chagrined.

"And your testimony," Tim responded, smiling apprehensively.

Bill knew when he'd been beaten, "I guess I don't have one," he admitted. "I always looked at being a Christian as living by the Golden Rule and putting others before myself."

"Coach," Tim said, "when fifty new players come and try to make the team and you know you can only put so many on the floor, how do you decide which ones to choose?"

"I give them all a chance to show you what they can do, then an opportunity to learn and grow, then I select those who show the most promise." Bill said.

"Anything else?" Tim asked.

"Well. they have to show a desire by showing up for practice and be willing to listen," he added.

Tim smiled. "God coaches the same way but has more room on the roster for players," he said. "The first step is that you have to come out and tell Him you want to play, then to be willing to listen and learn. Then He'll give everyone a jersey who sincerely wants to play on His team."

~   ~

They'd both graduated high school, she at the top of her class and Joel in the middle of the pack, but with several Universities scouting him as a point guard for their basketball teams. By now they had admitted their feelings for each other and had discussed life together after completing their education. What was troubling to them was the likelihood that they'd be forced to attend different schools, potentially hundreds of miles apart. Secretly, each was frightened that their passion may wane and die if they were not in frequent contact. That is often the test, is it the proximity that binds two souls together or is it something deeper and more permanent that will stand the test of time? As the summer ended and the fall semester grew nearer, each had made a commitment to a university, he to Ole Miss and she to CalTech.

"Will you marry me?" he asked, as they stopped walking and sat on a park bench under the shade of an overhanging tree. There were tears in their eyes when she said yes, but both felt an uneasy feeling encroaching on what should have been their time of greatest joy. The separation loomed like a rain cloud over their heads for the final two weeks before they boarded planes going in different directions.

Life at college was non-stop... everything. They tried to stay in touch but found it nearly impossible to maintain the kind of closeness they had shared while trying to adapt to a whole new life. Everything seemed so big when compared with home, the pace was frantic, and the days too short. When night came they were nearly too exhausted to stay awake and visit with each other. It may have been slightly easier for her because she only had a handful of things to juggle and she'd always been self-disciplined. For Joel, they almost made it sound like the reason he was there was to play ball, the school 'thing' was just a necessary evil.

Not that the coaching staff did not emphasize the importance of education, but they expected you to work it around practices, meetings, and game schedules and still keep the old GPA up. His first disappointment came when he found as a freshman he was third in a three deep competition for his position. What he had always lacked in speed he had made up for in savvy and shooting accuracy. But here, his teammates had that and speed as well.

When he called his dad feeling disappointed and expecting sympathy, he was surprised when Bill said, "step up your game, you got lazy here because the competition was lazy. You've got it in you."

That night Joel prayed for God to guide him and help him find the right place to fit in. Just the next morning at practice the coach took him aside and said, "we're going to give you a try at small forward, you're a good shot but too slow at point guard."

He wanted to argue but knew that the opportunity was a gift and his prayer had been heard. When Cassie called that evening he was actually excited to share the news with her. The world looked a little brighter, and their conversation a little less strained.

By the end of the first semester both Joel and Cassie were doing well academically, and Joel was sharing time with a junior at the forward position. He was surprised how well the transition had gone. Although neither family really had the funds to bring their children home at Christmas break they did anyway, and both Cassie and Joel learned a valuable lesson about how holidays work when you are a couple. They spent time with both sets of parents, celebrating Christmas morning with hers and Christmas dinner with his family. As their commitment to each other deepened and grew, they changed their previous plan to wait until graduation to marry.

They were married during spring break the following year with Cassie preparing to follow Joel to Ole Miss after their honeymoon. They stayed at the reception until dark before changing clothes to make the long drive to Aspen in the heavy spring rain. As they drove, their eyes grew heavy...

~　　~

In a time when men carried daggers rather than guns, it was an affront to watch a man's hands as you met him... it was foolishness not to. Dane Adams was the bastard son of aristocracy, living in the shadow of his half-brother, unable to take a place at his father's table. His beautiful mother, widowed by war, had become a servant, working in the kitchen, a woman paid but not well for her many services. The Duke had taken pity on the grieving widow and had given her the son that which her husband had not.

'Twas common knowledge among the servants of the Duke's sojourns into the bed chambers of those whose station did not allow them to refuse. Likely the Duchess was also aware, but chose to ignore it while she indulged herself with the young men of the court as well.

Dane had just turned twelve and served in the stables in whatever capacity his squire required, when the term 'bastard' made its meaning clear to him. That knowledge brought with it helpless rage and hate so fierce it soured his stomach. His father, the one whose name he shared, had also been of noble blood, but lacked the political connections to protect his holdings while away at war. It had been speculated that the Duke and his ilk had arranged for him to have been killed in battle for the very purpose of absconding with his fortunes.

The day dawned gray and overcast on the small island that would someday be known as The British Isles, threatening rain as it often did because of its proximity to the sea. A stiff wind blew inland from the east causing the young man to pull the collar of his coat up. His scrawny frame had little on it except muscle and sinew, giving his oversized shoulders and legs the look of a scarecrow as he hurried to his station at the stables. He knew that the squire would be waiting impatiently to assign him two days work and expect it to be done by nightfall.

There was no light visible in the stables as he approached, hope sprang within him that he'd beaten his tormentor to work this particular day. The familiar scent of the stable and its animals assaulted his nostrils as he opened the door and entered. Horses shuffled and moved within their stalls and nickered good morning to their keeper as they recognized his familiar footsteps.

"Get the muck out've the stalls," Dane heard just prior to feeling the fat hand of the squire on the back of his head.

There were twenty stalls and more in the long horse barn, over half of them were currently filled with horses. It was hot, thankless work to be done over and over without reward, the young man thought. It was a never-ending task to rake, shovel, and haul away the manure and soiled straw and wash down the stalls, only then to refill them with fresh straw and begin anew the next morning. The dozen or so horses who had the privilege of such treatment also needed to be groomed, fed, and watered, while others frisked in the green fields nearby.

Dane was tall for his age, but lean and spare like his father, the Duke. He had a narrow, hawk-like nose with large nostrils and smallish mouth which turned down at the corners. His hair was the color of flax and like his mother's, too thick to accommodate a comb. Unlike others of the commoners, whose features included round heads and square flat faces, the centuries of inbreeding among the aristocracy had developed a look of its own, unmistakable to anyone who took the time to notice. An angular face with high cheekbones and piercing eyes rounded out his features.

The previous occupant of the stall, having already been relocated to a clean one, Dane began raking the putrid mixture toward the opened door while fat noisy flies buzzed around his head. Sweat dampened his hair and ran down the back of his neck into his coarse woven cotton tunic. A small rickety wagon stood ready to accept its cargo, having been pulled out into the main hallway. The strong smell of urine and manure caused his eyes to tear up as he began to load the wagon with his three-pronged pitchfork.

"Well lad," the squire said cheerily, "it looks to be another hot one. We'd do well to get our work done early this day."

Dane thought to himself, "WE"? Who is this "we" to whom you refer, you fat lazy bumpkin, you haven't soiled your hands in a year. But of course he kept his thoughts to himself and his head down.

Chereval had been a French nobleman before being captured during the French-English conflict for supremacy, and relegated to servitude. He now served as head cook for the Duke and worked with Dane's mother daily. Schooled in swordsmanship and able to read and write, he became the father/mentor that Dane had never known. After most had gone off to bed, they'd often meet for a few hours of instruction in the use of the sword or the tedious task of learning to read and write. Dane never knew or asked where Chereval had acquired the two fine swords that they used. After each lesson both were carefully hidden away from prying eyes and greedy hands.

On his fourteenth birthday, Chereval pronounced Dane "adequate" with a sword and gifted him one of the matched set, but still kept it hidden in his quarters. Adequate was the term his mentor used to compliment his student without causing him to loose sight of his need to continue practicing the discipline and further improve.

While his half-brother dressed like a dandy, rode the stable of steeds into the ground, and forced his will on many of the working class lassies, Dane continued to live in squalor and work from dawn to dusk. Resentment became his constant companion, changing him from a carefree youth to a bitter young man. Chereval cautioned him often about how he drank the poison that was meant for another. His mother too had seen the change in her son as he was becoming all that he hated about his father.

As Dane held the stallion's head for his half-brother to mount, he took a slap of the reins across his cheek for letting it mince about. As Dane's eyes locked on his assailant, he could not hold his fury or his tongue any longer.

"You worthless dandy, climb down from that horse and face me before I pull you down," he said in front of a gaggle of townspeople.

Instead, William took the way of a coward and tried to run Dane down as he urged the horse over him and out of the barn. Over his shoulder he shouted, "you'll regret this day, stable hand, bastard, fatherless whelp."

The gathered crowd waited until the rider was out of sight before they cheered and gave Dane both nods and warnings. Within the hour word had spread to the town and among the servants in the main house. No one supposed that Dane would live through the night once the heir had told his father.

Chereval crept silently in the darkness, watchfully, until the side door to the stable was in his grasp. He held in one hand a sword and scabbard disguised in a bed sheet and a pillow case filled with food from the kitchen in the other as he pushed the door silently inward. As he peered into the darkened room, and before he could call out, a crude handmade dagger rested against his throat.

"Laggard, assassin," Dane whispered, venom dripping from his lips. "Your father'll not save you tonight."

"'Tis me," Chereval said, pulling back the hood from his cloak, "you were maybe expecting other guests?"

Dane let down his arm and with it the dagger that it held, while looking sheepishly at his friend. "One cannot be too careful of who comes a'calling in the dark of night," he argued.

"You'd be right about that Master Dane, and it'll do you well to saddle a steed and be on your way before others arrive behind me," the old Frenchman said. "Your mother has sent you some venison and fresh bread from the Duke's table, and I have brought your sword along with me."

"I thought to stand against him," Dane said, "fight him in front of our father and kill him like a dog in the street rather than run."

"You'll not have the opportunity to show your fine swordsmanship. If you stay you'll be dead by morning and food for the crows," Chereval admonished. "When the time is right, return and take what is rightfully yours."

Dane held the taller man close, imagining what it would have been like to have embraced his own father, then pushed him away and said harshly, "then be gone with you before they come and catch us both."

The mare was tall, nearly as tall as the stallion in the stable beside her, but she had more heart and was trimmer and faster than her lazy suitor. Dane had chosen her because it would be less likely that they'd notice her gone right away and he favored her over the others. A coverlet and a light saddle with a bag of grain and a wineskin were tied on behind it, the pillowcase across the pommel in front of him and the lanyard of the sword's scabbard across his chest rode lazily down his left leg as he walked her from the darkened stable and out under the starry sky. A scant few coins in a leather pouch were hidden inside of his vest.

They had not gone a furlong when a cry arose from the squire peering out from his quarters in the stable. "Who goes there?" he asked arrogantly, "what rights have ye to be mounted on one of the Duke's horses?"

Dane could not think of a good response so he kicked the mare in the flanks and disappeared into the night.

~   ~

Four years had passed, four years filled with both growth and disappointment, but Dane had endured where others had failed. He had lived the life of a vagabond while lacking many of life's skills, finances, and without comrades to cover his back. His spare frame had filled out with muscle and now served to give any who'd be inclined to roust him to have second thoughts. Always, always, the sword hung from his shoulder and across his chest as a warning that he was a man of action. Chereval would upon occasion hear of him from a traveler passing through and share the information with his mother.

The Duke had made no effort to find or punish him or retrieve the mare he had taken. Some supposed that possibly he was relieved to have the reminder of his infidelity gone and the mare was a small price to pay.

Because of his ability to read and write and his skills with a sword, Dane became the captain of the guard in Duchy in southern England where he rose to prominence and power. The Duke, an aging man of considerable means with only a daughter as his heir, took an immediate liking to Dane and treated him like the son he had never had. Much like Joseph in Biblical times who found favor with the Pharaoh, Dane ran the duchy with little oversight. In turn, he acted honorably and performed his duties with zeal and creativity. The old Duke's neighbors, who had anxiously awaited his demise, now saw their plans to divide up his holdings coming to naught. The mysterious young man who was now growing in both grace and wisdom held the castle firmly in his grasp.

Lorene, the Duke's daughter, was the singular gem in a tray of many, one to which one's eye would take notice and pick from the lot.

It was not that she was beautiful in feature and form, although that was also true, but more that she had a quality of beauty about her that was evident to even those whose sight had dimmed. Hard as the pommel of her saddle, yet as soft as the fine silk that lined her bodice, she could ride with the best and had a certain finesse with the foil that defeated many a superior swordsman.

Dane, much like the other young single men, was taken with her, but had the wisdom to steer a course that always kept them in the company of others and not alone together. He knew that because of his heritage and station, a romance born of passion and need would be their undoing. But, more and more their proximity to each other made them aware of their strong feelings which could not be ignored, so he spoke to the Duke and asked for her hand.

~ ~

"Joel, Joel look out!" Cassie screamed, shocking him back awake and into reality. He had been daydreaming until she spoke and looked up and into the headlights of the oncoming truck.

He died in her arms, his muscles quietly relaxing, the struggle for life ended, a smile rapidly disappearing from his lips. She opened her mouth to wail but no sound issued from her lips; grief consumed her, swallowing her up like the sea would swallow a small boat. Her mind felt almost vacant, disbelieving that what she knew to be true could really be happening. They had been married less than six hours, and yet their life together was over almost before it began....

The End

What if... Construction had not hampered your commute to work and the speeding car at the intersection had run the red light and had hit you broadside? What if that child had stumbled as he ran across the street without looking and had fallen in front of you as you hurried to your appointment? What if God was really not all-knowing and just let things happen randomly without His intervention?

The Birth of a Book

His anxiety level was running high as he sat down again before the old Dell XP, wondering what he would write. He had never written before, not in the sense that he would have expected others to want to read what he had to say. Yes, of course he'd written the mandatory stories required for English Lit and creative writing and had done well on those. He was an exemplary student with a brilliant mind, not that anyone would have noticed. What they saw was someone trying hard to be something he was not. He had no physical prowess, could not jump or run, and lacked the mechanical skills to participate in nearly every sport. He was a black-skinned Jew living in New York City named Jebidiah Silverstein.

Bible scholars have long speculated that many of the Jews in

Christ's time were dark skinned, possibly even some of His chosen disciples. But America and especially the hood in NYC had stereotyped what they expected from both races, and he was neither. Now it is understood by most that to be Jewish is to rigorously follow certain religious principles, it is also understood that it is very plainly a race that takes special pride in its birthright.

So then how did he dress and sound like a typical Jewish boy, while wandering down the streets with unruly black, curly hair? When he opened his mouth, most thought he was jivin' them, puttin' it on, as it were. Then at home among his own he was just as much of an oddity in the orthodox Jewish community, tall where they were short, black where they were olive-skinned, with a typical broad nose and ear to ear mouth full of white teeth. There's a saying, "you can take a boy out of the country, but you can't take the country out of the boy." It may be a little stretch but you can probably see where I'm going with this.

There he sat, before a blank white screen, its cursor pulsing like his beating heart, waiting for the first word to magically appear. A topic, he thought to himself, something interesting and entertaining that I know something about. That is about as far as he ever got, "something that he knew something about." Not that he felt he had to be the expert, but he didn't want to come across as uninformed and ignorant either. His life was mundane, uneventful, boring even, and a writer could not afford to be such.

Maybe a poem, he thought. I wrote a poem for my sixth grade girl friend, it wasn't that bad. But again no inspiration, he had no girlfriend now waiting to be impressed. Maybe something deep and spiritual he thought next, but then he wasn't that sure where he stood, spiritually speaking. The whole Jewish thing somehow didn't quite click with him and he knew very little about the "big church" religions. The "Mother

Mary" thing confused him all the more when he tried to equate it with God and Jesus. Yes, he did believe in God, of that he was certain, and even enjoyed reading the Bible although the second half, the New Testament, was technically out of bounds with his parents. He was unclear how God could be the "Father" that Jesus talked about, and yet say that He and the Father were one; the thing about the Holy Ghost literally blew him away. He had difficulty not thinking of Hollywood's rendition of ghosts and applying them as he read through scripture.

Jeb was sixteen, going on thirty, in a world that made little sense, where he felt mostly uncomfortable. He awoke with a start, his head on the keyboard of the computer and a sharp pain in his neck from being too long at a bad angle. He had fallen asleep while trying to formulate something to write worthy of the intellect that he'd been born with.

The cursor was still blinking with a long line of nnnnnnn's where his nose had depressed the key. A word, then several came to mind... *Take my hand and let me...* so he typed them onto the screen, then stopped until more followed... *show you.* Weird, he thought, this is like some kind of Ouija board thing only using a computer instead.

He was alert now, waiting for the supernatural message that he was sure would follow, but it didn't. He went to school feeling disappointed but throughout the day the words stayed with him, *"Take my hand and let me show you."*

Band practice ended at 7:00 and he walked the five blocks home to where his family was waiting patiently at the dinner table. He placed his kippah over his curly hair and joined them. Unlike most other American families, each meal was not a time of revelry and feasting but almost a sacred and formal affair. Little was said during mealtime in the Silverstein home.

Friends and even some family were divided, although not equally, into three groups concerning Jeb's heritage. Some supposed that for her own reasons Mrs. Silverstein had jumped the fence and found herself in the pasture with the wrong bull, to others it was a matter of concern and discussion, and to the few who knew that it was not her heritage that had spawned the dominant gene from generations before, but that of Mr. Silverstein. Apparently, somewhere, there had been a Jewish Ethiopian introduced into the bloodline and nothing more needed said. The Silverstein's had long ago tired of explaining the situation to those, most of whom, had already made up their minds anyway.

As the family dispersed after the meal, Jeb thanked his mother for the food and went to his room to do homework. As he sat down at the desk and signed onto his computer, the words that had haunted him all day returned. *"Take my hand and let me show you"* but this time a second *"Let me"* followed after. He began to type, *Let me show you, Let me... open up your eyes*, seemed to flow from his finger tips. He smiled to himself, the Ouija computer again. When nothing more followed he began his math assignment.

The house was quiet when he finished his studies, the rest of the family was already in bed and asleep. When he reached for the mouse to shut down his computer, another *"let me show you"* pushed its way into his head and joined the others on the screen. *Let me show you, Let me open up your eyes, Let me show you where to dig* appeared almost without effort. Jeb was stoked now, sure that someone from the supernatural was giving him a treasure map or something. After an hour, he went to bed and tried to sleep, but he could not.

Sometime, however, during the wee hours he must have fallen asleep because all at once his brother Levi was shaking him roughly and asking, "Are you going to get up or what?" He was tardy for his first class and after that, the day went quickly downhill. For all of the study he'd done the past evening, he'd seemed to retain little of it and felt certain he'd flunked his math exam.

At lunchtime he had no appetite and uncharacteristically did not join the crew to talk trash about the upcoming homecoming game. *"Where to dig"* he thought to himself, dig for what, treasure? The only thing he could think of that people buried was something valuable. His final two classes went by quickly, the bell signaled that students were dismissed to gather in the gym in preparation for the big basketball game with their cross-town rivals.

He sat in the bleachers, alone at first, then was joined by friends loudly decrying the prowess of the rival team. As the gym filled and game time drew near, both teams took to the court for drills and shooting practice. As he often did, he could picture his big tall black self on the court making the winning basket, an impossible dream for one so completely ungifted with coordination and ability.

A short pretty Latino girl, with sparkling black eyes and dimples to die for, took a seat just in front of him. She sat near him in English Lit and flirted openly with him on a regular basis.

"How come you don't go out dere and show 'dem boys how it's done?" she asked, trying to mimic the more apparent of his two ethnicities.

"Because I'm more valuable here holding down the bleachers for you," he answered.

They bantered back and forth for a few minutes before the teams left the floor and the band began to do its magic, making it impossible to carry on a conversation.

The shouting, the drums, the stomping feet and the cheers from the crowd did nothing to stop the words from parading across the screen of Jeb's mind, *"Where the living water lies."* Instantly it put itself together, *"Take my hand and let me show you, Let me open up your eyes, Let me show you where to dig, Where the living water lies."*

"Did you hear me?" she asked interrupting his trance, "some of us are going out to pizza after the game, do you want to come along?"

Maria's eyes were challenging him, teasing him, inviting him.

"Sorry can't, "he said. "I have a final first period in the morning and need to hit the books."

She pretended to pout then smiled and said, "I'll get you next time."

The inference was not missed on him, nor was the desire he immediately felt within his young body. Today was not the first time she had made it clear that she was more than a little interested. He laughed to himself when the reality of the situation presented itself to him.... just what he needed, a Spanish, Catholic, Jewish, black child to raise before he was even out of high school.

"Let me offer you direction" came the words that interrupted his fantasy, as clearly as if they had been on the big screen on the gym wall. Jeb felt kind of creeped-out now that he was beginning to see the lines of a poem coming together, and how appropriately the last line fit into what he'd just been thinking. How could anyone know the lustful secret that had just walked into his heart?

The game finally began with his team getting the tip off and taking the ball down court, only to loose it to a steal and eventually go down by two points. The lead see-sawed back and forth through the first quarter, with both teams near 20 points. At the half it was 36 to 39 with a trey at the buzzer to pull their opponents ahead. Maria moved up and took the open seat next to him and offered him some of her popcorn. He could smell her fresh clean skin next to him and the fragrance of some not so subtle perfume as she initiated a conversation.

"Don't know what you're missing," she said picking up the conversation where she had left off before the game began. "Everyone will be there and you can study anytime." She, unlike he, obviously had no desire to continue on to the University.

"I'm not much of a party guy," Jeb replied, "but it sounds like fun, I'll keep it in mind in case I get done early."

He had no intention of going but hoped that his response might placate her and she'd let the subject drop. He was feeling more and more uncomfortable by her presence and the feelings that he was experiencing.

"Let me offer you direction" at once filled his head as she continued to chatter beside him. The second half began with the home team pulling down a rebound and taking it home while drawing a foul in the process. Once again the score was tied at 39-all.

Maria must have tired of listening to herself talk because she made a production out of leaving and returning to her former seat. He had tried to be polite but was glad when she was gone. At the end of the third quarter his team started to pull away, by the end of the game they won by 12. Anyone who had not watched it would have thought it was a lop-sided victory.

The books under his arm felt light as the approaching evening breeze made him pleased to have worn a jacket. As he walked, he recounted the events of the waning day including the verses of the yet unfinished poem and his encounter with Maria. Many of the boys in his class had been bragging about their "scores" with girls since middle school. He had always assumed that most were wishful thinking or stretches of their imagination, but after his exchange with Maria, he wondered. Up until today, he had never given his virgin status a great deal of thought, but now it seemed an issue that needed to be addressed.

He was early getting home today and their evening meal was still cooking, his older sister Avigail was placing the plates and silverware on the table as he entered the room. He noticed for the first time how attractive she was and that somehow without his notice she had become a woman. He greeted them and went to his room and dropped his books on the desk, booted up the computer, and changed from his school clothes.

As he turned to leave the room, the computer screen caught his eye. There, where he had left off this morning was the message with the flashing cursor following a newly added line, *"Let me show you where to dig your well."* He was nearly certain that no one had touched his computer and certainly no one knew the message he had received at school just before the game. He was musing over it when his brother Levi opened the door and announced dinner. Levi and his brother Leib were twins

> *Take my hand and let me show you,*
> *Let me open up your eyes,*
> *Let me show you where to dig,*
> *Where the living water lies,*
> *Let me offer you direction,*
> *Show you where to dig your well.*

~   ~

Jeb's father Nathan was a tailor. Like the majority of those who lived in their neighborhood who bought, sold, cleaned, pressed or designed clothing, he immersed himself in his trade. He was what he did; he seemed nothing without the identifier which followed after his name. His mother Dinah was just that, a wife and a mother, a quiet presence that held their home together.

They lived in what was commonly known as a row house, much like the modern day condominiums of the western states, with a miniscule front yard and just enough room behind off the alleyway to park the family car, for those few families who owned them. Many were born, lived, and died in the same house that their families before them had. The twins were ten or eleven, depending upon which you asked, they were born just at the stroke of midnight New Years Eve and one always claimed to be a year older than the other when it suited their purpose.

As always, his father asked God's blessing upon their food and that it be sanctified to them before they began the ritual of eating. The twins, as usual, had to be reprimanded before the meal had ended for their irreverence and the poor table manners that came with their age.

After dinner they spent an hour formally studying scripture together before being released to their homework.

"Father," Jeb asked as the others dispersed, "why do we no longer have ritual sacrifice?"

Jeb knew enough about the disputes between the Jewish community and the Christian one to know their answer but wanted one from his father.

"My son," Nathan said quietly, "our sacrifice was offered up to God since ancient times in accordance to instructions given to Moses for forgiveness of our sins."

Jeb nodded respectfully, then asked, "Yes Father, that I know, but why did we stop, are we still not sinning daily?

Nathan could see that his son was trying to understand what was lacking in their refusal to accept Jesus as the sacrifice for sin. Obviously he had been encountering an outside Christian influence which led him to question what he had been taught. As he struggled to explain, much he supposed, as his own father had many years before him, the stubbornness of their people to accept the new covenant. Possibly his struggle lay in his own unsatisfaction with the answer which he himself had been forced to accept as a young man.

"When the Temple was destroyed," he began, "we had no place, no way to continue to offer animals as atonement for our sins. Each was forced to address his sinful nature privately in prayer to God and ask for forgiveness."

While that much of it made sense to Jeb, it seemed incomplete and not in keeping with the strict laws of their beliefs. "How," he asked, "is one to be certain that God hears and accepts our repentance? And… do we not continue to sin immediately after praying? Must we do it over and over our entire lives just to be assured that we are forgiven?"

Nathan felt uneasy, much as he had as a youth, uneasy that for all of their truth the answers did not put him at ease and draw him close to God. "Let us sit with the Rabbi and ask these questions of him," he said deflecting the responsibility. "Perhaps he can explain it better than I."

With that Jeb was dismissed and the matter closed until another day.

Back in his room, with more questions in his head than answers, he tried hard to concentrate on his homework, but failed. He turned to his computer which, like a pet dog, seemed to be faithfully awaiting his return. Jeb was not unaware as he reread the lines of the poem that it held a significantly spiritual tone. He went to his closet and removed the Holy Bible from its resting place and turned to the first book in the New Testament, Matthew. An hour passed as he read and re-read the passages and tried desperately to visualize the pictures painted in his mind by this disciple of Jesus.

He felt disloyal to his father but also compelled to continue as Mark retraced many of the steps of the first book. They were contemporaries, friends, and colleagues even, telling the same account from slightly different perspectives. It became clear to him that they had not copied from one another as some claimed.

The house had become still as he laid down the book and returned to the computer. Another line had been added, *"Put your trust in me my child"* and then another, *"You'll have no fear of hell."* He nearly went to find someone to verify what he was reading because he was questioning his own sanity now.

> *Take my hand and let me show you,*
> *Let me open up your eyes,*
> *Let me show you where to dig,*
> *Where the living water lies.*
>
> *Let me offer you direction,*
> *Show you where to dig your well,*
> *Put your trust in me my child,*
> *You'll have no fear of hell.*

There it was, clearly in print, staring back at him waiting for him to assimilate it, consider its message, and believe. It was after midnight and he knew that he should shut off the lights and rest and yet he could not. He reopened the Bible and coursed slowly across each page and into Luke, the one known as the doctor. He noticed a different style as Luke told for the third time the story that was now becoming so familiar to him.

He was feeling emotional as he read about his friend, his Creator, and his God being unjustly tortured and killed yet again. A lump welled up in his throat and his dark eyes threatened to loosen their load of tears down his mahogany cheeks. Another line presented itself to him, *"You'll walk the streets of glory"* seemed to begin the next stanza, and behind it another that seemed to complete the first... *"You'll never walk alone."*

Tears were now running freely as he considered the message that he had just been given, sobs of sorrow mixed with joy shook him. An invisible hand completed the message, *"For those who are called to my side, My Father calls my own."*

> *Take my hand and let me show you,*
> *Let me open up your eyes,*
> *Let me show you where to dig,*
> *Where the living water lies.*

> *Let me offer you direction,*
> *Show you where to dig your well,*
> *Put your trust in me my child,*
> *You'll have no fear of hell.*

> *You'll walk the streets of glory,*
> *You'll never walk alone,*
> *For those who are called to my side,*
> *My Father calls my own.*

Jeb hit the print key then saved the poem to his docs file. A strange feeling came over him, warmth, a feeling of being overfilled with joy, a feeling of comfort. He knelt beside his bed and prayed to receive the promise that had just so recently been explained to his heart. Jesus came to him, wrapped him in His arms, held him close and told him of His never ending love, of the plans He had to unite the races, to bring them to Him.

In God's time and in God's way His will be done, more about Jeb later.

The End

The Conversation

"Are you alright?" a voice asked.

I opened my eyes and looked up from where I was sitting on the grass with my back against a tree.

"Yes, I'm fine," I answered, trying to see the speaker in the fading glow of the setting sun.

"It's not always safe," he began, concern apparent in his voice, "your watch and... things" he continued, his voice trailing off.

He did have a point I thought, it was already dusk and I had been sitting alone in a now nearly deserted park for several hours.

"What are you doing?" the ragged looking man standing in front of me asked.

"Listening," I replied.

"To whom?" he asked, noting that no one was nearby.

"Listening to God," I answered.

He smiled and said, "Does He talk to you too?"

"Sometimes," I answered, returning the smile, "You?"

"Oh yes, often so loudly I look about to see if others have heard also, sometimes He wakes me in the night with a few words that I need to hear," he continued.

"How do you know it's God?" I asked him, having often wondered the same of myself.

He smiled again and answered, "I just know. It's so different when He initiates the conversation."

I nodded, knowing well the feeling he had described.

"Mind if I join you?" he asked as he sat on the grass nearby without waiting for an answer.

He looked unkempt but not dirty and the excited glow in his pale blue eyes disarmed me to the point that his presence held no menace.

"Sure," I said, as though he had waited on a reply, "it will be nice to have company. You live nearby?"

He smiled, showing a prefect set of white teeth, "on the street," he said as though that were a house address.

I took special note that the word 'homeless' hadn't been spoken. "Oh," I said, "where do you stay at night?"

"God always provides," he answered vaguely.

We sat there for a few minutes in silence together watching as the sun finished its arc across the heavens.

"We should go," he said, standing up as though we were traveling together.

I stood wondering if and why I should be following his lead, but then gathered my things together and fell into step beside him as he walked back toward the lighted pathway that coursed through the park. The lights of our small town beckoned us toward them.

Without thought I asked, "have you eaten, it'd be nice to have company for dinner if you'd join me."

He smiled, then said, "You don't have to. I mean, I have money, I can pay my way."

I knew that I'd come dangerously close to judging him by his appearance and assuming he was indigent. I also knew that self-respect was a fragile but important thing among those who had little else.

I returned his smile and answered, "Either way then, but I'd still like to have company and resume our conversation."

We walked together to where the park ended and asphalt began. Most of the stores still remained open hoping to attract shoppers on their commute home after the work day. A block ahead on the left corner was an ancient neon sign that flickered occasionally but read "Café." As we neared, I noted that I had never noticed it in the fifty years that both it and I had been on this corner. Through the windows I could see a scant half dozen seated inside, some eating, others talking and drinking coffee. We went inside without discussion, as though this had been our predetermined destination, and took a booth along the wall.

"Do you eat here often?" I asked, while looking across the old Formica'd table at him.

"I never have," he answered, "but it smells good and looks clean."

It had a homey feel to it too, which I had noticed the moment we crossed the threshold, like most little mom and pops that served the same clientele for years, until they all became like family.

"Coffee?" the waitress asked, while already turning over the cups and beginning to pour it.

"Yes, thank you," we replied as one.

"Menus?" she said while handing us each one.

"Thank you," we replied as we opened them and began to scrutinize their offered faire.

"Meat loaf looks good," I offered, pointing to the picture on the right hand page. "Chicken fry too."

He nodded in agreement and continued to read. Finally he nodded as if agreeing with himself and said simply, "pot roast."

Of course I had to look back at the menu to see what I'd missed and continued until I found the pot roast. Now I had created for myself a dilemma since all three entrees sounded immediately wonderful.

Our waitress returned, refilled the nearly full coffee cups and stood holding her order pad waiting for us to speak. She looked to be in her mid-thirties, with dark brown hair and a hint of gray already finding its way in. A little over five feet with dark brown eyes, and a round face. I noticed no ring on her left hand and wondered if she was single or divorced.

"Pot roast, if you please," my new friend said quickly, "and a glass of water without ice."

"It says that the pot roast comes with vegetables," I said, "could you tell me if they were cooked with the roast beef or separately?"

She smiled and answered politely, "Cooked together just like mom used to make, that's where the flavor comes from."

"Well then, I'll have the same and a glass of milk," I said.

"Will that be one check or two," she asked

"One will be fine," came the quick reply from across the table, "And," he added, "I'll take it."

I started to object but could tell from his smile that I should accept his hospitality so I just replied, "thank you."

"And," he said with a flourish, "You are very welcome."

~ ~

While we waited for the waitress to return with our meal we sipped our drinks and appraised each other without talking. I found it difficult to guess his age or heritage, both eluded me as I tried to find the telltale markers that were usually apparent. I finally settled on a number somewhere between thirty and fifty and guessed maybe either Spanish or Middle Eastern but could ascertain little by just looking.

"Have you lived in the town long?" I finally asked, in an attempt to regain the closeness we had shared in our first moments together.

He must have known I was trying to draw him back into conversation because he smiled before replying, "No, this is my first visit. And you?"

"I've lived here all of my life," I answered. "Born and will probably die here," I quipped.

"What do you do when God speaks to you?" he asked seriously.

"Do?" I asked. "I'm not sure what you are asking."

Our waitress returned carrying small dinner salads and a saucer of warm rolls, before he had a chance to answer.

I felt uncomfortable not knowing who should or if we should bless the food. Looking across the table I could see he had bowed his head and was already quietly asking the Lord's blessing upon it without invitation or fanfare. I bowed mine also and ended with an audible Amen, mostly for his notice.

He looked up and smiled before taking a roll and pulling it apart and adding butter. I did likewise and ladled one of the three dressings from the holder on the table onto my salad before adding my customary salt and pepper. Neither of us attempted to speak as we enjoyed our salads and fresh bread.

"I try to listen," I said, answering his question of ten minutes previous, "then depending upon what He said, try to obey."

He nodded while forking his last bite of salad into his mouth.

Our waitress returned with our meal and refilled our drinks, and asked if she could bring us other condiments. We deferred and she left our table. Across the room, an elderly couple had finished their meal and was sorting through their pockets to combine their funds to pay their bill. A young man sitting alone watched them carefully then rose quietly and walked to the cashier where he laid down a few bills and spoke quietly to the woman behind the counter before leaving.

A radiant smile filled my new friends face.

"There are many others who hear His voice also, and obey as well," my companion said, "but often do not recognize from Whom they have been inspired."

I guess that I missed his point although I did agree with what had been said.

"It is difficult," I responded, "to always know, to always understand what we are being told. Don't you find that true as well?"

The carrots and potatoes were delicious, bathed in the natural gravy from the meat and seasoned just right with the added flavor of the cooked sweet onions. The roast was tender and juicy as well, but fell to second behind the veggies as my palate savored their combined flavors.

"No," he said pausing before finishing, "I do not share your nature to know why, therefore it is easier for me to just do what I'm told."

I immediately wished I had the faith of this man, that I could accept without question like Abraham had, and not second-guess what I thought I'd heard.

Across the room, the old couple seemed to be arguing with the cashier about their bill. I perceived that they were short of cash and reached for my wallet and started to stand. My friend put his hand on mine and shook his head from side to side without speaking. I settled back into my seat.

He left a substantial tip on the table before we stood and approached the cashier who was shaking her head and smiling.

"No charge," she said as we neared, "it's already been taken care of." Then she looked right at me and said, "Your debt has been paid in full."

He smiled and pressed a bill into her hand before closing it and looking over his shoulder at a young couple who had just been seated in a booth with their two young children.

"And, theirs as well," he said.

As we walked back to where we had first met, I felt a melancholy a sort of loneliness that was now hard to explain.

I took his hand and asked, "Will we meet again?"

He answered, "I am certain we will."

The stars overhead had come out and were dazzling in their brightness, the moon, now a white orb, cast its reflected light upon the darkened landscape. All seemed right with the world. I turned toward him to share my appreciation of its beauty, but he was gone.

The End

The Means to Murder

In just under a year he had completed eleven assignments, had banked nearly a half million dollars, and had helped the nation in its search for a return to solvency. He was a patriotic man but not unaware of the dangers associated with his job. He had learned in his Ivy League college the values which still guided him and allowed him to see the "greater good" in what he did.

Sixteen seemed insignificant to him in the face of the looming failure of the nation's retirement system, but still sizeable if you threw in the expense of the Medicare system on top of their monthly retirement benefit. He wondered also, how any others were duplicating his efforts in large and small cities across the nation.

Another thought crossed his mind, how had he been chosen? Certainly the organization had the full resources of the Social Security Administration at its disposal, most likely contacts within the CIA and FBI also, if not the Oval office. Leadership near the top had organized and financed the project with access to insider information.

His first selection had been a retired General of strong conservative persuasion, a "double dipper", who still held considerable sway within the military ranks and in Congress, a fine choice he thought. At sixty-five he would begin to add thousands a year to his already more than adequate military retirement, and further burden the system as his needs for medical care increased with age. Who knew, with free health care he might last another twenty years.

He smiled to himself as he remembered how the tough old bird had swam to the bank and made an attempt to crawl out of the water. A single kick to the face had changed his mind as he then slid into the murky depths. He was not a trained or sophisticated killer, but he was resourceful and determined. He had first chosen a darkened stretch of highway, paralleled by a canal on the preferred route home from the officer's club where the General made his appearance each Tuesday night.

He had just waited quietly while several drinks were consumed, then at the right time had nudged the rear corner of the General's car, just enough to cause it to spin out of control and into the water, a maneuver which he learned watching a cop show on TV. That should have been enough were it not for the old man's training and stamina. But no telltale skid marks from his vehicle would cause investigators to look any farther than face value.

It was not right to say this was his "first," actually his grandmother held that distinction. But of course that was many years ago, although his motive had been the same. His parents, second generation Germans, had owned a small bakery in New York. At age five he had been orphaned by a junkie wanting money for a fix. His father was shot when he attempted to "throw the bum out," and his mother also when she came screaming to his aid. His grandmother and only living relative lived lavishly in Manhattan. No one knew for sure where her money had come from, but they suspected it came across the Atlantic with her as she fled the occupation at the end of the war.

If not Nazi, her manner and air were surely that of one. She believed in their ideals. She made sure he knew he was a "necessary burden" and that his "expenses" always exceeded his orphan's benefits. He suspected that she always pocketed much of it before his needs were met.

Having just turned eighteen and graduated high school, he made sure his presence in the front yard was witnessed by his neighbors. Then, slipping quickly around behind the house and in the back door, he made certain she missed the top step as she started downstairs, age and gravity did the rest. She lay dead at the foot of the stairs with her only heir standing emotionless over her.

He had never known love and had never felt the love of another human being. He quickly returned to the front yard and made his presence known, striking up a conversation with a passerby, then suddenly turned his attention to the house and asked, "did you hear a scream?"

Racing to the house together they found the old lady. With no reason to suspect wrongdoing, the investigation was over and done quickly. He went off to college where he quickly found a group of like-minded individuals and joined the Young Democrats and participated at every opportunity in protests against capitalism. He found it popular and profitable to hang with the rich and idealistic, he aligned himself with them as his own fortunes dwindled.

Someone's wealthy father always had a place for him in a high paying, low responsibility position, treating him like a son. Through his connections, his number never came up in the draft, as he continued to be schooled in the art of living well.

Now in his mid-thirties, he had never held a real job and with grandmother's fortune long since spent, and rich friends avoiding his calls, he began to face the reality of his circumstance. In desperation he joined the re-election staff of a New York congressman where he excelled and rose to prominence. After the landslide victory, he was offered a staffer job in Congress, where he made still more valuable contacts. He rode high for a time, moving in powerful circles for several years until a bid for re-election failed, leaving him without work or friends.

It was then the call came. The caller explained that he was a friend of an acquaintance, and just mentioned the potential of an opportunity without details. The liaison had spent a great deal of his time delving into his political leanings, his social values, his family ties, and especially his willingness to operate just under the radar, slightly outside the framework of established law.

Curious but far from stupid, he was aware this was a black-ops kind of organization and choose wisely not ask questions. At first he was tested with small but necessary tasks like stealing mail from prominent right wingers, eavesdropping on conversations at political fund raisers, and reporting back with any impropriety that might be used later against them. He prepared detailed dossiers on nearly all prominent conservatives and their escorts, including pictures which might hold the opportunity of later blackmail.

By the time the second call came, he had enough insider knowledge to know there was a higher calling waiting somewhere for him, a position where he could serve the "greater good". He was sure there were other eyes watching when he was 'interviewed' for his new position in this special service. He felt that every question had been carefully worded, his answers graded and psychoanalyzed. Every nuance in his posture or speech pattern carefully noted. His passion for his country, his hatred of the wealthy, his disdain for blue collar workers, and the vision of helping to remake America, made him a perfect candidate.

With a minimum of visible guidance and oversight he would

receive each 'selection's' information by courier and likewise a sum of cash after the process had been completed. He had no guidelines as to when or how the job was to be done and no way to make contact to ask. He was aware that since 9/11, transactions in normal banking institutions bore careful scrutiny and therefore established several personal accounts under assumed names.

Not having the expertise to secure good forgeries on the black market, he elected to use names and Social Security numbers from the deceased. He then secured picture ID's from warehouse stores, private gyms, and credit card companies, and created his own Social Security card on the computer. He made it a practice to frequently make small deposits and withdrawals until he became well known to the staff and they no longer required identification. Face recognition increased and so did the deposits, but he always stayed under the ceiling of $10,000.

He was aware of several things as he struggled to become an assassin. It was apparent that none of the selections had a husband or wife, all were approaching or at their golden day of retirement, and all were or had been upper crust wage earners, and thus would soon be drawing large monthly government checks. Most were single to avoid scrutiny by a grieving spouse and to eliminate the payment of survivor benefits.

His second selection was the widow of a wealthy dry cleaning franchisee who lived alone but spent more than a fair amount maintaining the illusion of her youth at spas, salons, and in the company of youthful, paid, personal trainers. He felt no qualms when he hit her in the darkened crosswalk with his already damaged vehicle. By midnight his car was lying at the bottom of the East River.

He'd waited a day or two to report it stolen. It seemed now that his employer was convinced of his reliability for his payday was increased. He also noted that any surveillance he may have been under had been withdrawn, for they now simply called to confirm when the work was done. Apparently he had proven himself.

During his off time, he busied himself reading crime novels, interestingly they became his instruction manuals. He also started frequenting bars and became familiar with the suppliers of drugs, liking the idea of the date rape drug, where he could watch the victim's reaction as he plied his trade, without leaving any sign of force.

Number three hardly qualified as murder, since he was already on life support, having been a victim of an auto accident. It appeared however that he could exist in his current state for many years while drawing substantial medical benefit, in addition to his SSI. Uncle Sam was paying for 24 hour nursing care and for the prescriptions which arrived nearly daily at the house.

Supplied with a mislabeled bottle, he easily substituted it for the original, while the care giver was in the shower, it caused an almost immediate MI. The blame would come down on the pharmacy which was heavily insured, but with no heirs to push the case against them, little would be done.

The choice of number four was nearly his undoing, but hardly his fault. Maude, a well-to-do widow of many years, was nearing her 65th birthday, showing no signs of winding down. She appeared vital and full of energy as he rang the bell, causing him to have second thoughts about just smothering her with a pillow. He knew she would not die easily and he cautioned himself to take it slow and wait for the right opportunity.

He had come, briefcase in hand, as representing an insurance firm with investment information for her to consider. She ushered him into the living room and offered coffee which he readily accepted, noting that he would need to remove all finger prints before he left.

He had just begun his opening about funding her retirement when she interrupted saying, "John should be home any minute, and we have agreed to make these decisions together."

Caught off guard, he asked politely who John was.

"Oh," she replied. "I am sorry, John is my husband, we've just been married a little over a month. After all these years widowed, it doesn't come easily to think of myself as a married woman again."

His mind racing, he recovered quickly, noting that he had would very likely have been caught in the act by good old John given a few moments more.

"Congratulations", he nearly shouted, straining to sound sincere, "I am so happy for you both. But," he added, "this will change the whole proposal I had prepared for you, I'll need to make an appointment for another time."

Closing his briefcase and standing, he headed toward the door. Yes indeed, his plan for her had not included a husband. He'd have to mention this to his contact, suggesting they double check their information before giving him an assignment. Just as his hand closed on the door knob, it turned, he found himself nose-to-nose with the recent groom.

Frustrated again by the whole encounter, and with another witness who had a clear look at his face, he smiled warmly offering his hand, "you must be John", he said.

"Yes, John Musgrove, Maude's husband," came the reply, "and you?"

Slipping his phony business card, with ink hardly dry, into the waiting hand he answered, "Cameron Smith, Security Mutual Retirement Funding" sounding as smooth as butter. "I had planned to show Maude some of our options but hadn't realized she'd remarried. With your permission, I'll reschedule with proper information for you both to consider, at a later date".

"Please do, but call ahead," responded John. "She and I can't afford to let grass grow under our feet at our age, we try and stay busy."

As he returned to his car, the possibility of getting caught overcame him. His prints were all over the house, two credible witnesses had seen both he and his rental car. Neighbors and others could have as well. This would not do, not at all he thought.

On the drive home, as he calmed down, he congratulated himself that he had taken time to think ahead and print a business card. The address on the card was one digit removed from the real address of an existing company. The phone number rang into a cell phone which referred it to the fax number of one of his banks. He was quite sure that anyone attempting to reach him would give up after getting a repeated busy signal at the bank or the annoying fax sound in their ear.

He entertained his first misgivings about his new career, and saw for the first time, a retiree with potential to lead a meaningful life. Fortunately, his second thoughts were short lived, he refocused on the "greater good" principle that acknowledged that some must be sacrificed for the good of the many.

Later that night he received the call, questioning why the assignment remained incomplete. Slightly irritated by the tone, he attempted to turn the tables, blaming them for providing inaccurate information.

Just as he was going to elaborate, the voice posed a question, "Were we wrong about you? Did we make the wrong choice? Are you one who questions orders and makes excuses?"

A pregnant pause hung in the air, and then he resumed, "I am sorry to come across so strongly. We were impressed with your past work and supposed you would improvise when you came across little bumps in the road."

Taken off guard and feeling a little threatened, he fawned more than he would have liked, then responded, "I'm sorry, it's been a long day, and I admit I was unprepared to handle the situation involving a healthy strong man when I expected a little old lady. I'm still learning."

"Very well," came the reply, "we are all learning. Make sure the job is complete within the week."

"But, but..." he stammered, "there's no reason now that she's remarried, her husband would continue to get her partial benefits and his own as well."

The voice was clipped when it came back immediately, in a tone that left little room for discussion, "take them both." The voice on the phone continued explaining, "the decision has been made and there is much more to this than just Social Security benefits. They pose a hazard to our organization and our nation."

When the dial tone sounded in his ear, it gave him a hollow feeling in his gut, for the first time in his life he felt fear. What had he gotten himself into?

His drug connection proved resourceful when he asked about the purchase of a firearm, showing no emotion as he produced the small pistol. ".22 Smith," he offered, as he went quickly over its features, "you know it?"

"No, never held a gun before," was his answer.

"Thought not," said the pusher with a sneer, "you don't look the type. Good gun in close, semi-auto, you just point and pull the trigger until it clicks. Then, if they're still standing you take off running. It wouldn't hurt to spend a few minutes at a range before you depend on it to save your life."

He added, "the gun's clean, that's worth another $200, so I need $1,500 total."

As he counted out the bills, he got a free history lesson, "Same caliber that almost took out Reagan. It's small but deadly, no recoil, nice and quiet."

He had read in some of his novels that the little caliber was preferred by professional killers, who liked the fact that it could be fitted with a silencer and was light and easy to hide. When he returned home, he changed clothes, and examined his purchase, loading and unloading it until he understood its workings. With it unloaded, he worked the safety and dry fired it several times as he 'killed' the announcer on the weather station. Satisfied with its simplistic design, he made the decision to return tonight and finish his assignment. Somehow it never occurred to him that he could miss his target, it looked so easy on television.

He rented an older dark green sedan for one day, from a seedy lot. With cash up front, they did not require a credit card. As he left, the man pocketed the cash along with the folded rental agreement. As he had hoped, if the car was returned undamaged, there would be no paper trail for anyone to follow.

He parked just around the corner, away from the street light, killed the engine but hesitated to get out for several minutes. He took the time to remove the bulb from the courtesy light while he organized his thoughts. Then with great care, he worked the slide action, putting a live round into the waiting chamber, and very gently slid the safety into place. His heart raced with anticipation at what he had just committed himself to do, both fear, and power, flowed in his veins.

Although the plan included leaving no finger prints, he had taken precaution to wear gloves. In the movies, they always chose black as had he, with an unmarked ball cap pulled down to obscure much of his face. His oversized light jacket belied his true build and accepted easily the burden of the little Smith. He was tempted to smile as he left the vehicle, but concentrated on suppressing his glee while walking slowly down the sidewalk. It was now just after ten o'clock, the block was nearly dark, with just an occasional bulb burning in a living room or bedroom here and there. A retirement neighborhood, he thought, right to bed after the news.

He had carefully loaded the clip at home with twelve bronze colored hollow-points' he had done a mental run through of the scenario. First, approach the darkened porch quietly, unscrew the single bulb, then a gentle knock on the door. He was unsure of using the doorbell so elected not to do so. Beyond that, he was on auto pilot, having no knowledge or control of the next string of events.

Once on the porch he knocked three times and waited, then followed it up 30 seconds later more aggressively. A light came on, shining dimly down the hallway, followed then by another, in the living room. He could hear footsteps and the deadbolt unlocking as a voice asked, "who is it?"

"Police," was his reply. "Is everyone alright in there? We've had a report of a break in."

Just as the doorknob started to turn, he grabbed it hard and shoved the door inward knocking the man into the room. They had but seconds to exchange looks and the Smith barked three times, mid-section, chest, and throat from just feet away. The older man slumped without a sound to the floor while a scream issued down the hallway from the bedroom. He was at once surprised and pleased by the ease of it all, making the length of the hallway in four steps. She had not even left the bed, but sat up with eyes wide as fear turned to hatred.

"You", she lashed out with venom in her voice, and then attempted to rise.

Three more times the Smith spoke sharply, with the first round hitting the headboard, the second and third impacting her chest and shoulder. She fell back, but was not dead. Her eyes burned like coals into his soul. He moved in closer and left a single red spot on her forehead.

Although seeming loud inside the house, he observed that the weapon had not caused a light to come on in either of the two neighboring houses. Adrenaline coursing through his veins, he mentally congratulated himself while enjoying a cold, selfish smile. No motive to follow up? Good question.

Then the thoughts of his previous fingerprints came back to mind, the coffee cup and the business card. The cup, along with hers and a few dishes were in the sink and the card lay on the counter in plain sight. Washing all the dishes quickly and pocketing the card, he felt quite efficient, as a man in control of his own destiny. He did not need their money but took the wallet, watches, jewelry, and her purse anyway, after putting them in a handy plastic grocery bag.

A quick look around the back porch yielded a gas can with a few inches of fuel left in it. He took care not to spill it on himself, he poured a few ounces into a metal bowl and put it in the microwave and then set the timer for five minutes. He had stolen the idea from an action movie, and hoped Hollywood had based the movie on fact. After pouring the remaining gas around the kitchen, then the carpet and sofa, he left by the same door he had entered.

He walked purposefully but slowly down the sidewalk and returned to the waiting car. He could hardly sit still and could not resist the urge to drive slowly by the house. Just as he reached the corner, a flash of light answered the question of his improvised bomb's effectiveness. Within seconds flames were visible and lights had begun to come on in the neighborhood. As he eased away, he mentally added numbers four and five to his resumé.

The following morning he got up late, spread cream cheese on his bagel, and prepared himself a double espresso, then sat down with the morning paper. He hadn't made the front page, but there were several nice pictures on page 2 of the fire, with a half column saying little more than their names and that the fire was under police investigation. He knew that investigators would easily determine that the fire was a cover-up for the murders, but also had nothing with which to tie it to the other murders.

He reasoned that any attempt to profit from the other goods he had taken would leave a trail back to him. So he burned what he could in his backyard barbeque and relegated the rest to the storm drain several blocks away and watched as it slid under the muck and debris. The gun, what about the gun? The voice of caution told him to dispose of it also, to write it off as a cost of doing business. But, he loved the power it gave him, the feel of it, and the authority it commanded. He decided to wait and think it through more thoroughly before making a final decision.

He refilled his cup for a second time, and reached his phone on the third ring. The "voice" on the other end that had now become as familiar as an old friend, said simply, "nice work."

He felt redeemed and yet humbly replied, "thank you, it worked out well."

"We'll be in touch," was the answer as the line went dead. He felt elevated and could hardly wait for the next call. It was in his blood now, he no longer feared but enjoyed the challenge.

Number six was somewhat unique in that he had to develop additional skills and duplicity to achieve it. The target was a very wealthy man, living in the secure environment of a penthouse with cameras, security locks and armed security personnel. He reasoned that both the person and his possessions were the focus of this protection, with all access denied to unknown visitors. As he read novels and books he learned that surveillance and planning were to be necessary if he were to be successful. This was a job which should have gone to a more well trained professional. He felt honored and eager to justify their confidence in him.

The man, E. J. Casey, a retired CEO several times over, lived alone but still held positions on many Boards, and led a very active life. He had a schedule to which he adhered that made his movements predicable, a very good thing.

The target was easily brought up on the computer, which also provided an interesting snapshot of his life. It was intimated that there was a possibility that he had stepped down as a result of beginning dementia or acute depression after the death of his wife. He was a card carrying, conservative Republican, traveling in the highest circles with great influence in both business and Congress. This insight, while useful, offered him no clear direction as to how to access the man. He began to shadow him, following the limousine from the entrance of the building to its return later in the day, taking copious notes, and then staying with the limo back to its garage.

He found it interesting that the man had chosen not to own the limo, but leased it and its driver. Probably a tax benefit he surmised, letting the government bear the burden of his extravagance on the backs of the poor. He had learned to hate the rich back in college while at the same time envying them.

The chauffeur looked as much a body guard as driver and seemed ever vigilant in his duties. He could have easily been ex-military by his carriage and conduct and not a man to be easily outwitted or over powered. E. J., as those close to him were allowed to call him, enjoyed a massage and steam three times a week, frequent luncheons with friends or business associates, and an occasional evening meal also, sometimes to include a stage play or opera, but never alone. He appeared to be trim and fit, not a heavy drinker, and showed no interest in female companionship, while leading a solitary but privileged life.

The dealer seemed to take amusement in his request, "rohypnol? You mean roofies?" he questioned. "Sure, so you are trying to score without a lot of foreplay, is that it?"

Not at all amused, he remained composed, then asked, "tell me about how it works."

"Just a little in their drink, they lose control and don't know what hit them. You score and they never know you were there. Doesn't leave a trace in the blood stream either," the dealer volunteered.

"Anything else I should know?" he asked.

"No," said the dealer, "only take care what else they are on, it can be a killer too."

"That right? Like what else?" the assassin asked.

"Let me write it down for you, I don't want you to be bangin' a corpse" laughed the dealer again. "You get a chance to shoot the Smith yet?" he questioned.

"No," he lied, "been a little busy, maybe next weekend. So, how much for the roofies?"

"On the house if you bring me some pictures", he laughed, "otherwise $50 but still cheaper than a hooker." They exchanged a Benjamin and walked away, both smiling.

He now had half of a means, but still needed opportunity. He dared not try and get the second half of the cocktail from the same dealer or he'd be as much admitting his purpose for it. He wanted to keep the source open without revealing too much about himself. But, to find another willing to fill the need discreetly bothered him some. He began to frequent other bars, vigilant but quiet until he picked up on who was most popular with the younger crowd. Watching for several nights, he finally sat down near the fat Spanish-speaking dealer who was quietly nursing a beer.

The place was nearly empty when he finally spoke, "drink amigo?"

The man half turned, eyed him, and then pointed without speaking at his glass. "Gracias."

He motioned the bartender over and pointed to both glasses, then without a word laid a $100 bill on the bar. After several rounds, he tipped the bartender $10, then slid a scrap of paper face down over to the thirsty Mexican. Turning it over, then looking him up and down suspiciously, he nodded, placing his fat hand over the $50 and remaining change on the bar.

"Mañana" was his only reply.

Having little choice but to trust the dealer, he nodded, "Si, mañana." He paid for one more round, then left.

He waited until later the next evening before he entered the bar again, he failed at first to see the Mexican. This time he took a seat in a booth with his back to the wall and a good view of the room. Out of his element, and frightened, he had brought "Mr. Smith" along, just in case he might need company. After a few minutes and couple of drinks, they locked eyes and the dealer nodded, tipping his head slightly toward the rear entrance. He returned the nod, then hesitated for a few moments, finished his beer, and quietly moved toward the door.

He waited in the alley for several minutes, until his eyes became accustomed to the darkness. When the door finally opened the dealer and two companions walked silently into the darkness.

Swallowing his fear, he moved toward them, his hand tightening on the Smith inside his jacket. "You have something for me, señor?" he asked in a voice sounding much braver than he felt.

"Si", was the reply, the Mexican held a small bottle toward him. His two amigos held their ground speaking softly to each other. He left his hand in his pocket, with the barrel of the Smith just showing a profile under the jacket, his other hand closed over the bottle.

"Gracias", he offered while backing away and keeping a watchful eye on the three.

"De nada", he replied the answer as they backed toward the door. He waited until the door closed behind them and then realized that he had been holding his breath, and let it out with a relieved sigh. They apparently had been just as afraid of a trap as had he, but had held no malice toward him. Lesson learned, his luck had served him well this time, but he would have to be smarter and more prepared in the future.

As he entered, it was apparent to him that this was not a front for prostitution or some low class massage parlor. At the counter he also found that the client list was exclusive and allowed no room for "walk-in" trade from the street.

The young woman at the counter eyed him carefully, and then asked, "excuse me, do we know you?"

"Regretfully, no," he offered, "I am just in town for some meetings and E.J. suggested I might find a little relaxation here."

"Oh, yes, Mr. Casey is a dear friend whom we treasure", was the reply, a new warmth crept into her voice. "It will be an hour before we can make an opening for you, is that acceptable?"

"Yes, certainly, I feel foolish for not calling ahead," he answered.

"Not a problem in the least, please follow me while we make your wait more pleasant," she offered as she led him down a short hallway and into a spacious and lavishly furnished parlor.

"May I offer you a Perrier or perhaps a cocktail and something light to eat?" she said, as it was obvious that she was giving him, by association, the VIP treatment.

"What does E.J. usually enjoy? I'll have the same, thank you", he replied.

"Mr. Casey most often just has Perrier with a twist followed by a steam, and a deep tissue rub." she said as she placed the drink beside him.

"I'm Cameron Smith, most call me Cam", he responded, looking her right in the eyes. She was a beautiful woman, maybe mid-thirties, 5'6-ish, with long auburn hair, self-confident and very poised.

"Thank you, Mr. Smith. I trust you'll enjoy your time with us and your trip to New York. I'll add your name to our preferred client list to avoid future embarrassment," she said, returning his gaze.

With tip, it came to a little over $400 for a very pleasant afternoon indulgence, but well worth the investment. He may well have created the opportunity that had hereto not been available. He also had taken note that the water had been opened, then poured in a crystal glass with lemon, prior to serving. Both the glasses and the ice were very accessible, as was also the beverage cooler. He'd buy some of the same brand name water, doctor it up at home, make sure the seal didn't show damage and simply substitute it for theirs. He noted they only chilled a few at a time.

Friday was E.J.'s next regular day, he held a standing 2:00 appointment for which he was always punctual. The driver had always remained with the car, parked at the curb reserved for guests. "Cam" showed up 20 minutes early for his own 2:00 appointment and pretended to have misread the time and was shown to the parlor once again. As soon as his hostess retired, he quickly emptied the two remaining bottles out and replaced them with his own, thus limiting the choices to one. Then, he waited another 5 minutes, returned to the desk feigning illness and laid $400 on the counter to cover "any inconvenience" and promised to reschedule at another time.

He had just stepped onto the sidewalk as the limo pulled to the curb and parked, the door opened and E.J. disembarked. As Cam waited in a nearby coffee shop sipping his latté, it took less than 30 minutes for an ambulance with lights and sirens to arrive at the spa.

He finished his cup and walked nonchalantly across the street, and joined the gathering crowd of onlookers. After another few minutes, the EMT's reappeared pushing a gurney with the subject draped with a sheet. It was loaded and left without lights or a siren, indicating to him the need for haste was past. The morning paper confirmed that number six was in the history books, the cause of death was listed as apparent heart failure. He could not help but smile, congratulating himself on his resourcefulness. He looked forward now to each successive assignment, viewing them as a test of his ability to overcome obstacles.

Several weeks passed before the call came. In that time he became nervous and restless, wondering if he had done something wrong, he worried about having had no contact. Even the sizeable stipend which had been delivered had not quenched his desire to perform. However, when the call did come and he heard the name, fear overrode his elation, number seven was a former Republican Governor whose name had been mentioned as a potential presidential candidate. Knowing better than to argue with the caller about the choice, he did ask however about the time frame.

"As soon as possible, of course," was the reply, "but certainly before the Republican caucus".

That left several months before any substantial extra security might be assigned to the prospective candidates. His techniques continued to be improved with each mission, he elected this time to create for himself a new persona. He shelved his contacts and started wearing his old wire rims once again, he let his hair grow and had it styled over his ears. These changes served to broaden his face, giving it a more rounded appearance while aging him a few years. He considered a beard or mustache but discounted them as being too radical.

He also changed his style of dress resorting to a buttoned down look, which gave him the appearance of an accountant, bookkeeper, or academic. As Cameron Smith, he became a notable presence at Republican rallies and fund raisers, to the point of first name recognition. Though they knew little about him, they did not hesitate to cash his well-placed contributions, and never questioned his loyalty. As the caucus neared, the several hopefuls started keeping higher profiles, glad handing, and mingling with their supporters in an attempt to solidify their base.

As he continued to increase his contributions, they became notable enough to earn him a seat at the front table among the movers and shakers. It was on this occasion that he was seated beside Dane Adams, former governor of Ohio, his target. He guessed Dane to be in his early sixties but looked fifty, having had his hair touched up and expertly trimmed, his clothes professionally chosen and altered to slim his waist. He had little doubt that this man was a front runner among the candidates or that no expense was being spared to make it seem so.

Although it was always hard to tell when speaking with politicians, he seemed sincere and devoted, and although their ideologies were far apart, Cam came to like him. It was little surprise then when he received a personal invitation to the Adam's mansion for a fund raiser.

Cam arrived slightly late and gave the crowd time to mingle and enjoy a cocktail or two before he entered unannounced. He had taken note of the security cameras at the front gate and of many others which ceaselessly scanned the grounds. There also were presumably armed security, discreetly positioned over the entire complex. Those who were obvious had the confident look of men expertly trained to handle any situation which might arise, much the same as had Dane's driver.

Cam had gained entrance at the front door without further scrutiny by virtue of the gold embossed invitation, but knew also that the cameras had recorded his arrival and that a later visit would receive more individual attention. Having no idea of what security he might encounter, he had left his friend Smith at home, and likewise his supply of roofies. This was to just be a recon mission he told himself.

After laughing and talking with the other guests, he was able to complete the circuit of the entire ground floor, he made an excuse when he intentionally entered the kitchen area to take special note of its service entrance.

A partially opened closet revealed an inventory of the starched white uniforms which the kitchen staff wore. Just outside of the expansive wall of windows, which lined the rear of the house, was a well-lit fountain and shimmering pool, covering well over an acre, with cabanas and wet bars skirting its perimeter. The crowds were here also, drinking and talking, in small knots enjoying the warm evening. These were the "wanna-bes" that were significant enough to warrant an invitation, but hardly fit in with the crowd inside. Mostly younger, they were trying to establish themselves as movers and shakers by their transparent laughter and off color jokes.

Cam returned to the graying, more self-assured crowd inside and struck up a conversation with a group which included the host. He nodded at appropriate times and offered just the right amount of opinion to be relevant, but tried to remain cordial and reserved. A slight nod from Dane as they locked eyes, established him as part of the "special ones". He returned the nod, then moved on to another group where he tried to seem interested in their conversation.

He continued this pattern until he was sure his presence was noted by many, then left as he had come in, adding his envelope and check to those in a bowl by the front door. Unsure of what would be notable among the rich, he had written it for $25,000, hoping that it was but a small investment in a big future payday.

In a seedy pawn shop on the east side he had made it clear that he was against deadly force when the clerk had suggested a firearm, but did feel the need to protect himself. The suggestion came, as he had hoped, that he might consider a taser unit. Something that would disable without killing and had no federal paperwork to file.

It contained a high voltage discharge capacitor producing low amperage, and was small enough to carry in a pocket. Inexpensive and effective, it held a single drawback, you needed to be close to the subject. The electrodes had to make contact to work. Of course he had read all of this at length on the computer prior to shopping. The salesperson was telling him what he already knew.

The police used a unit which propelled a contact to the subject that delivered the charge by means of a lanyard, allowing them to stand several feet away. His choice however, was one the size of a TV remote that needed to make contact directly with the subject to deliver the charge. As he turned the corner, leaving the shop, he purposely chose to walk down the dark side of the street. Vagrants and bums inhabited the darkened doorways, dealers and pimps cruised the streets, as shuffling masses came and went. He was apprehensive, knowing that his clothes identified him as a target, but continued to walk, his hand on the taser in his pocket.

A hand shoved him roughly into the alley just as he approached it. A menacing voice demanded his wallet. As the man's acrid breath filled his nostrils, he jammed the weapon against his chest and squeezed the trigger. The man gasped, fell without a word, and lay jerking on the ground. Cam smiled, kicked him as he passed by, and then returned home. Once again he had the 'means', now to provide just the right opportunity for himself.

He found, that like E.J., Dane was also a creature of habit, who felt the need to appear organized to his constituents. His typical day included six quick laps in the Olympic sized pool, followed by a steam, a massage, then coffee while he read the Times and Post. By the time he had finished, his trophy wife had made herself beautiful and joined him for a light breakfast. They had no children of their own, his two from the first marriage were at college and seldom home. His staff included three domestics, a chef, and four rotating security guards. During the day political staffers, friends, and cronies came and went in large numbers.

Cam had found that Dane was a collector of artifacts, being especially fond of Middle Eastern treasures. Since these were now protected by law in most countries, the black market was filled with items large and small, dating back thousands of years. Covertly, Cam secured a small Egyptian vase which supposedly had housed spices needed to make the afterlife more enjoyable for some minor ruler. He called Dane on his throwaway cell and asked if he might drop by with a gift and was granted the privilege to join him for lunch at the mansion.

After making himself conspicuous to the security detail who

waved him in and to the other guests who were already there, he asked if he could present his gift privately, feigning humility. They retired to a private office, but when Dane saw the prize he was so overwhelmed he forgot discretion and proclaimed his prize to the waiting group. Cam held back, pretending embarrassment and then joined with them in the revelry.

Cam waited two days, then approached the front gates with confidence, which he did not feel. "Dane is expecting me", he lied as the gate swung open without further dialogue.

It was early, therefore he was shown to the pool area by the maid. He could see Dane swimming the pool in long even strokes. As she turned and left them, Cam noted they were alone, but under the watchful eyes of the cameras. Cam walked to the near end of the pool, and hesitated by the ladder, Dane made his turn and swam toward him. He could see recognition is his eyes and as a smile brightened his features, he began to swim toward Cam. Dane had just grabbed the two gleaming chrome tubes and was beginning to lift himself upon the step when Cam plunged the taser against his chest. As he re-pocketed the weapon, Dane's eyes rolled up until only the whites showed then he slipped silently under the water without a sound.

Cam exited the house quickly, restraining himself from running, returned to his car, and left without being questioned. In an area less populated, he ran over the device with his car several times and then dumped the broken fragments into a storm drain. He stopped at a nearby shop and had his hair cut into its original style, and took off his glasses, then replaced his button downs with sport clothes and put in new colored contacts which completed the transformation.

It was nearly an hour before the body was discovered and several more before it was determined to be a homicide. The camera angle did not clearly identify the type of assault but did show some device being thrust at the victim. Although they had a suspect and pictures, there appeared no record of a Cameron Smith matching their description. Vehicle plates proved stolen from a different vehicle and police were left with more questions than answers.

Because of the stature of the man, his prominence in politics, and his wealth, the FBI assumed it was a professional hit. Now that Cam had entered the ranks of the big leagues, he regretted that he had paid little attention to his fingerprints. He knew that since he had never been arrested, in the military, or been fingerprinted they would be a dead end, but if he were ever a suspect they would be conclusive evidence. What resources the FBI could bring to bear were beyond his imagination.

When the call came, it was with congratulations, a warning, and a million dollar payday. He told them he needed a vacation and some help setting up an off-shore account. Surprised when they agreed, he was heartened to find a passport, new identification, and a ticket to Rome in the name of "Roger Williams" delivered to his home, with an access number to his new account.

Landing first at Heathrow in London, then boarding a connecting flight to Rome, he settled into the seat, then closed his eyes and began to evaluate his life. For the first time he began to question the direction his life had taken. He had never been with a woman, although it wasn't like he hadn't thought about it. It had never been worth the trouble to get emotionally involved with the possibility of being betrayed. But now, he began to wonder if he shouldn't pursue some selfish indulgence.

With money beyond expectation, without strings to hold him, he could learn to enjoy new pleasures without the risk of being hurt. Just the thought of it gave him a new sensation which cried out to be satisfied.

Yes, he would make that a priority he thought to himself, taste in full measure the pleasure which Italy had to offer. All at once he questioned, why Rome? Was there a purpose or reason to their choice of destination? Did they have a motive? All at once fear overwhelmed him as it had in the beginning. He hated the feeling of being out of control.

He had enjoyed an ordered, structured life, where things were predictable. But that of course was gone now. Exciting as it was, he still longed for the security of having control. Another thought had been nagging him also, how does one quit? It was obvious you couldn't just retire and walk away. Would they ever allow him to stop? He hardly thought so. More likely he'd just disappear with no one to question or care. Live for today, he thought, and for the joy of the chase.

He must have dozed off because the Captain's voice caused him to jump. They were circling, waiting for their turn to land in Rome. He felt like a child, having never traveled, speaking no foreign language, and not at all streetwise. He felt panic rise within him. Could he survive here? Time would tell, but then he really had little choice, did he? He felt that he had moved too fast, too quickly, far exceeding his still developing abilities.

Then, all at once, he had a plan, a plan to grow and learn from competent instructors. He had read about mercenary training camps throughout the world that discreetly catered to the rich. He was rich, wasn't he? Yes, quite so. He would think of this as a well-earned vacation and learn the new and necessary skills he needed to survive.

With his carry-on in one hand, while pulling the larger bag behind him, he moved toward the exit where buses and taxis lined the curb. Several limos with drivers stood discreetly in an adjoining area, one held a sign which read "R. Williams." As he neared, the limo the driver nodded slightly as he compared a photo with the face then said, "welcome to Rome, Mr. Williams. Allow me to take your luggage."

Wow, this was first class treatment, he thought, as the door opened for him. Inside, the limo was as big as some motel rooms, with natural wood polished to a sheen, plush upholstery, bar, and television. He was relieved when the driver, who spoke English with a very slight accent, pulled away from the curb and announced their destination in the form of a question, as though he assumed "Mr. Williams" knew where he was staying.

Cam/Roger replied simply, "yes, thank you." In a very professional, but friendly tone, the driver asked if he had been to Rome before and then if he'd like to see a little of the city before checking into the hotel.

"Yes, that would be nice, if you have the time," he answered, almost shyly.

"I am at your service for the length of your stay, sir", the driver replied, handing a business card over the seat. "You can call at your pleasure, any time."

As they drove, they talked, the driver not only hitting the famous landmarks, but also giving him local color information.

"Women?" Cam asked.

The driver answered, "Yes, of course, I can help with that also Mr. Williams".

He felt like Alice in Wonderland, whatever he wanted seemed within his reach. All of a sudden he felt hungry, and realized he had not eaten on the plane.

"Is there somewhere we could have dinner?"

"Yes, of course, what do you enjoy?" the driver queried him.

"Whatever you recommend is fine, will you join me?" asked Cam.

"As you wish, thank you", he efficiently responded. Williams noted that he would have to resist the urge to become this guy's buddy. Stay friendly but keep a respectful distance between them, he thought.

As the driver bent to open the door, Williams noted the presence of a weapon concealed in a shoulder holster inside of his jacket. So, now he had his own security man, he mused at the irony of it, and then reconsidered, for what other purpose the driver may serve.

Over their dinner, Williams found that Lonzo, as he preferred to be called, lived outside the city proper, was single, and lived alone. He offered little, but answered when asked without hesitation. He had apparently been born in Northern Italy but preferred the warmer climates of the south. Williams guessed him to be mid-thirties, an inch or so taller than himself, maybe 6'2" and around 180.

Finally, while enjoying dessert, Williams patted his own jacket in the armpit and asked, "necessary?"

The reply came quietly, "sometimes", without further elaboration. Williams understood that further questions concerning the weapon would be out of line.

At the hotel, Lonzo delivered the luggage to the expansive front desk, addressed the concierge in Italian, who then produced the room key with a grin, bowed and said, "Mr. Williams, welcome, please let me show you to your room."

The driver slipped some Euros into his waiting hand and also addressed Williams. "At what time shall I return, sir?"

Cam, who was still operating without a plan asked, "can I call you?"

"Yes, of course," came the quick reply. "I'm about 20 minutes away".

In his room, Cam marveled at its opulence. As he unpacked, he formulated plans to buy some clothes, enjoy the cuisine, and let Lonzo deliver up the promised women who would tutor him in their arts of pleasure. Far in the back of his mind was the nagging thought that there would be another call, another request, and another "selection." He was in no position to complain or refuse and he knew it. They owned him.

It was 2:00 p.m. local time when he awoke, disoriented and still tired. After a hot shower, pastries and coffee which had somehow magically appeared, he opened the drapes and gazed out over the street from the 5th floor. He felt good, better than he had in years, as he dialed the phone to the driver's home.

Lonzo picked up on the second ring. "Sir?" was the single word reply.

Williams was caught off guard that it was known who was calling, but managed, "Yes, I am ready whenever you can be here."

"Very well sir," he said. "Fifteen minutes if traffic is light," and then came a dial tone.

Williams reasoned that Lonzo must be hired exclusively as his driver and that any incoming calls would be from him, or maybe they had caller ID over here too. Williams took several thousand Euros from his carry-on before committing the remainder to the hotel safe, as he passed through the lobby. The limo was already at the curb waiting for him by the time he exited the building. Although the driver was still in uniform, he looked much more relaxed and friendly than the previous night. Perhaps, thought Williams, he got laid last might.

"Lonzo", Williams asked, "do we have an agenda, you and I? I mean, have your employers given you instruction concerning me?" That was as point blank as he could get and still sound in control.

"Sir, I'm not sure what you are asking," he answered. "Do you require more than a driver?"

"No," answered Williams. "I was just wondering about what kinds of things you may be able to help me with. I have been reading about certain kinds of 'camps' in Soldier of Fortune Magazine and find them intriguing," Williams offered. "Do you have knowledge of them?"

Hesitating a few moments, Lonzo replied, "yes, but not first hand. Would you like me to make some discreet calls?"

Playing down his excitement, Cam commented. "If you have time, it might provide an interesting additional dimension to my vacation."

Dropping the subject, Lonzo asked, "is there somewhere in particular you'd care to go today, or perhaps to see?"

"The countryside, somewhere that you'd enjoy, I can see the city anytime," Williams answered.

The driver seemed pleased at his choice, just as Cam had hoped. He had planned to form a bond with the man which could transcend their current financial relationship. As the city fell behind them, first hills, then mountains came into view, the expressway became a country road. He could just feel the tension leave his body as he enjoyed the scenery.

"Is the same kind of area where you live?" Williams questioned.

"Yes, just a short distance ahead, perhaps you'd like to see it?" Lonzo answered.

"That is very generous of you, I'd love to, if it is not an inconvenience," he replied.

"Not at all", Lonzo answered. "I seldom have guests."

They traveled in silence for several minutes before the car turned right onto a private road which led up to the house. Williams had no preconception of what to expect, but was more than surprised by what he saw. The house looked more like a California estate than a bachelor pad, of Mediterranean design, but not far removed from the Spanish look common to SoCal. The estate was on a flat, backing into the hillside on two sides with the third tailing off steeply down the canyon, which they had just ascended. Red tiles lined the roof, whitewashed brick or stucco the exterior, showing contrast to the rounded doorways trimmed with natural wood. The courtyard boasted fountains and statues but no grass. Several trees, maybe olive or fig, offered shade and dimension to round out the landscape. He saw no signs of human life but a large dog of questionable breeding that came out to meet them.

Williams had waited for the driver to open the door for him, feeling a little foolish for having done so, and then was introduced to "Claudius Maximus", or Max as he was called, who seemed pleased to see them. Max stood nearly three feet tall at the shoulders, on long muscular legs, no doubt having the ability to take down an intruder if he had chosen. But with his master in attendance, he wagged his tail with joy and affection.

"May I offer you refreshment?" Lonzo offered, with what seemed genuine enthusiasm, leading them through the front door.

"Certainly, if you will join me," Williams replied. "And... will you call me Roger?"

Lonzo hesitated, pouring them each a large glass of dark red wine, then simply nodded and said, "Roger."

They drank in silence for a few minutes, with Lonzo carefully watching his employer before he gestured around the room and said, "please, let me show you around."

Each room was large and well decorated with items that seemed to hold special significance to its owner. Lonzo pointed to or touched each, with personal affection, as if introducing a friend. It was very tasteful and clean but showed no female influence. Williams wondered if there were women in his life.

As if reading his mind, Lonzo offered, "I have a housekeeper in twice a week and an occasional overnight guest, but have never been married. It makes my life much easier to manage."

Cam nodded. He could feel the bond beginning but decided to play it slow and careful.

"Myself as well, life can get too complicated if we invest too much in another," he offered. "What do you enjoy?"

A broad grin came but disappeared just as suddenly as Lonzo recaptured his reserve. "Solitude, good wine, clean air, exercise, sailing, a willing woman without too much wit or principle, and of course a good romp with Max, here... a simple life."

Instantly Williams envied him. He had a full rich life and did not know it. Maybe he too could learn to live well and yet simply as his new friend seemed to.

They finished their glasses and filled another, walking out the rear doors into a courtyard at the back of the house. The view was stunning, natural vegetation green and lush covered the adjacent hillsides. To the south, hazy in the distance, he could barely make out the blue expanse which was the Mediterranean Sea. Its influence, no doubt, accounted for the rainfall which produced and maintained the green hillsides. Some 100 feet away, carved out of the hillside was a bare square of earth with a target centered in it.

As he stared, his concentration must have been noticed because Lonzo, in an offhand manner asked, "do you shoot?"

"Just a little," was Williams' reply, while suppressing a smile which the image brought to mind. "Though I'd like to learn more," he added.

"Then we shall!" came the response, accompanied with a childish grin and a refill of the waiting glasses. It was obvious that Lonzo was enjoying himself and wanted to show off a little to his guest.

Although considered a 'purse gun' by American standards, the .380 Beretta Model 86 was quite a weapon compared with Mr. Smith who had been left at home. It held eight rounds in the magazine, each looked to be triple the overall size of the .22 rounds. The gun featured a tip up barrel which allowed the first round to be manually loaded. He liked that. It was simplicity and sophistication in a single package.

As Lonzo affectionately handled the gun, pointing out its features, he did not realize that he was also giving good, first hand instruction. Williams took care to observe but to show restraint while absorbing the wealth of knowledge provided. When asked what brand he preferred he simply answered "Smith," having no knowledge of the model or caliber.

When offered the gun, Williams deferred to his host saying, "no, your gun, your home, I'll just watch and learn."

Lonzo shrugged but did not hesitate, he assumed the shooters stance and quickly squeezed off the full clip into the waiting target. Laying the gun on its side on the nearby table he motioned to Williams to join him. Together they walked to the target. Williams noted that all but two of the rounds had hit the bulls-eye and they, only by a fraction of an inch, had fallen outside.

"Your turn, my friend," said Lonzo, returning to the table and reloading the clip. He seemed to be showing the effects of his third glass of wine.

Williams knew that there was too much to remember and realized that an attempt to fool his host would fall flat, so he simply played the man's ego in saying, "only if you'll teach me."

Gladly Lonzo assumed the role of teacher, showing every detail from how to hold the gun, how to stand, sight, and squeeze the trigger. He allowed Williams, "Roger" by that time, to go through the ritual several times before he chambered a round and snapped the clip into the butt. Carefully reaching around Roger, he released the safety for him, readjusted his stance and backed away, leaving Williams to squeeze off four rounds before he knew what had happened.

Lonzo returned to his side, carefully helping him to remember to keep the muzzle pointed down field, and continuing to coach and instruct him. Williams realized that after the first round, he had closed his eyes and just pulled the trigger completely missing the target. Lonzo did not criticize but rather showed him how to concentrate on the target and not the gun, to look through the sights and see the target only. By the second clip, Williams had two rounds in the ring and three more on paper.

Although Lonzo did not shoot again, he did continue to load and reload for Williams, coaching and critiquing him time and again until the box of 50 cartridges was gone. By the last clip, all rounds had marked paper and half within the bulls-eye. When the two liter bottle of wine was also gone, the men returned to the house walking and talking like old school chums. Roger had never shared such comradeship. Being a loner all of his life, he had enjoyed the time more that he could have described, but lacked the initiative to tell his new friend.

They had shared another glass of wine with antipasto when Williams asked, "does your country have restrictions on gun ownership as we have? Is it possible for a visitor like myself to buy such a gun?"

Lonzo appeared drunk, but something in his eyes indicated he had heard and taken interest in the question. "Yes," came the answer slowly. "We too have regulations and paperwork, but most of that disappears with the application of a few Euros. Those are the 'papers' which seem to get things done."

Williams did not push the issue. The driver had made it plain enough that a gun could be had if the price was right, just like at home. Feeling cordial, Williams asked if Lonzo had a favorite restaurant, he was feeling the desire to treat his companion to a nice meal. The reply came with Williams realizing that he had insulted his friend. He had cut short the offered hospitality, giving the impression that he was ready to leave.

So he quickly added, "I am having such a good time, I hate to go back to the hotel".

The timing just right, the smile returned to the Italian's face as he replied, "how about we see if I am as good a cook as a marksman?"

Pleased with the offer, Williams agreed and finished his glass. And so the day came and went, darkness fell, but they continued to eat and drink until finally falling to sleep in their chairs.

Williams awoke to bright sunshine, the smell of food cooking and coffee brewing. Lonzo was busily moving about the kitchen humming and showing no ill effects of the previous night, while the American felt like he had needles poked into his eyes and his sweat socks in his mouth. Max lay nearby watching the activity with soulful eyes but not making a sound. Following a plate of Eggs Benedict with fruit, bread, and several cups of black coffee, Williams finally was able to speak.

"Thank you, my friend, for a wonderful day and great food, I have never enjoyed myself so much", he said with true sincerity.

The driver smiled, then replied, "So... what would you like to do today?"

"You mentioned sailing", Williams offered. "Perhaps we could both enjoy a day on the water, have you your own boat?"

"Yes, replied the driver, a modest one, only 15 meters, but quite sturdy and with accommodations for four."

After a quick stop at the hotel to check for messages, a hot shower, and shave, Williams was driven to a shop nearby to purchase the correct attire for the day's adventure while Lonzo hit the market for wine and groceries. Lonzo had replaced his uniform with leisure attire and had dropped all pretense of subservience. Williams joined him in the front seat as they drove south toward the coast, asking questions and getting his bearings, while Lonzo pointed out points of interest along the route.

It felt as though two close friends were sharing a holiday together. Finally they parked in an area designated for those who rented slips and docked boats nearby. Lonzo led the way with arms full of provisions, and Williams followed behind equally loaded, they passed through the secured gate with a swipe of Lonzo's card and proceeded down the long dock.

Several hundred feet later Lonzo stopped, and swung several of his packages over the gunwale of the waiting boat before he stepped aboard. As Williams handed his burden to the driver he was breathless at the beauty of the craft, gleaming with polished brass, chrome, and waxed to a brilliant sheen. It was obvious that Lonzo took great pride in his boat.

Lonzo opened a hatch, revealing a short stairway into the lower section of the boat. Arms laden with packages he stepped below, immediately beginning to stow the provisions away. Williams had never been aboard a small boat but saw immediately the need for organization and thrift of movement when in such cramped quarters. He waited topside until beckoned by Lonzo to join him below.

Efficiently, Lonzo took each package and put it in its proper place before taking another from Williams. When finished, the captain turned to his guest, gesturing around the compact cabin and said, "welcome!"

As they shared a bottle of red wine served at room temperature Williams became familiar with the boat's amenities. The kitchen area, or "mess", as Lonzo called it, and the "head" or bath, were very compact and functional, but the two staterooms were spacious and well appointed. Two couples could sleep very comfortably in them for a few days. Lonzo told him that he always packed provisions for three days for every day he expected to be at sea just to be on the safe side and water enough for a week.

Although the Med was not like the Atlantic or Pacific, it was far too large and treacherous not to be taken seriously. While Lonzo expected to be in complete control of the boat, he still took precaution to make Williams familiar with it and to explain the functions of the necessary rigging, steering, and support systems.

As the day moved toward the noon, Lonzo breached the subject of female companionship, not being pushy but suggesting they might make the trip more interesting. His misgivings tempered with wine, Williams had agreed, much to his own surprise. Delighted, Lonzo indicated he'd make a couple of calls from the marina and return shortly.

Williams was left alone to explore and evaluate the upcoming adventure. Just over 72 hours ago he had left the States under duress, with misgivings about his future and no idea of what it held for him. Now, he was settled in, had learned to shoot, made a friend, and if his luck held, was about to get laid for the first time in his life.

It was less than an hour when Williams heard voices and saw Lonzo, with a beautiful woman on each arm, coming toward the boat. Both tall and slender, in maybe their mid-thirties they seemed at ease with the situation. One with thick auburn hair dressed in swim suit overlaid with a light robe carried only a large canvas bag while the other, with raven hair had a backpack thrown carelessly over her shoulder.

Williams wondered instinctively if they were prostitutes or just available acquaintances of his new friend. Not that it mattered to him at all, he could learn from them the arts of love the same way he had learned to shoot from Lonzo. While neither woman spoke English well, both were able to understand it. The auburn beauty had grabbed his arm and with a kiss to his cheek, claimed him as her own, while Lonzo with a smile had chosen Lena and poured each of them a glass of wine to toast their voyage.

In less than thirty minutes they were under sail and moving away from land, a light breeze blowing through their hair as they gathered on deck. Lonzo handled the wheel like an expert as they left the harbor heading out into open water. He made small adjustments to the rigging here and there to get full advantage of the wind. Williams guessed the temperature in the mid 70's or low 80's, with a cloudless sky and dark blue water. Neither woman seemed a stranger to the sea, both standing facing forward, holding onto a lanyard to maintain their balance, chatting in their native tongue and laughing.

Lithe, sleek, athletic and full of vitality were the adjectives which came to mind as Williams observed them. He began to feel aroused by thoughts of what might lie ahead but wondered if they would somehow know of his virginity. He had done well on the range by holding back and letting the more practiced marksman take the lead and show the way. He found this strategy appropriate here also. He'd let Alta show him what pleased her and then find pleasure in doing so himself.

They sailed throughout the day and well into the gathering dusk before losing sight of land, passing many islands along the way. Finally Lonzo dropped the sails and made them fast, laying anchor at 250 feet in gently rolling swells. The women went below while the men rigged the marker lights fore and aft, and then lighted the mast. When they went below they were pleased to find cheese, salami, crackers and filled wine glasses already on the small table with two laughing women seated waiting for them.

As quickly as Williams was seated, Alta pressed herself against him, allowing him to feel the heat of her breast through the thin fabric.

She kissed him full on the lips, then pulled away taking his hand in hers. Across the table Lonzo and Lena were also kissing but keeping an eye on he and Alta. Suddenly, Williams could feel Lena's bare foot in his crotch as she smiled demurely and moved her toes, giving him a wink. Alta, not having missed the performance, slapped her foot and scolded her in Italian while using her own hand to take its place.

It was not necessary to understand her words to understand their meaning. She took his hand and led him forward into the darkened stateroom before closing the door behind them. Their clothes fell away almost of their own accord as they laid back on the soft bed. As he had hoped, Alta took the lead, showing both expertise and enthusiasm for the task at hand. When they finally fell back into each other's arms, they were damp with sweat but filled with the ecstasy which unbridled passion had brought them. He could not help but think that years of deprivation had not diminished, but enhanced, the act. How much more wonderful it had been than between two pimpled, sweaty teens in a car's back seat.

They did not speak, they just held each other, hearing the lapping of the waves against the hull of the boat. They alternately dozed and re-consummated two more times that night. When they awoke they could hear activity in the galley, where Lonzo and Lena were talking and starting breakfast. Pancetta, the Italian equivalent of bacon was frying in a pan, coffee was beginning to drip, filling the space with its aroma, and heavy coarse bread had been sliced and dipped in egg in preparation of frying.

The couple moved as if they had cooked together all their lives, anticipating each other's moves, which was necessary due to cramped working quarters. Williams thought their practiced moves were not unlike the sexual encounter he had enjoyed just hours before.

The next day was a repeat of the first, alternately sailing, eating, drinking and indulging each other's needs. Lonzo allowed him to steer the boat, patiently explaining the nuances of it. While a motor boat was similar to driving an automobile, the sailboat required constant vigilance and adjustment to maintain safety and take full advantage of the breeze. He could easily see the need for a hand or mate, as they were called, on large sail boats or when on rough seas. But he did well keeping the boat's heading while watching the compass as he had been instructed, until Alta moved up behind him, pressing herself against him. With a smile, Lonzo took the wheel as he and Alta went below to re-explore each other.

Later that night, Williams awoke, alone in the cabin. As it always is when secrets are whispered, they always make our hearing and concentration become more acute. The three of them were talking in low conspiratorial tones about him. He moved closer to the door, picking up the thread of conversation. His new friends had apparently been hired to keep an eye on him until a decision could be made as to if and when his services may be terminated. They were basically keeping him incognito, away from the prying eyes of the FBI and others who might cause them harm.

Fear gripped him, and then anger. How could he harm them? He knew nothing, his employers had made sure of that. But, of course he was a loose end and the stakes were high, he knew he had little chance of seeing Rome again. There was discussion as to how it should be done without reaching consensus, but the three were in agreement that it was necessary.

Williams returned to the bed, his mind afire with thoughts and schemes, desperately attempting to formulate a workable plan. He was physically no match for Lonzo, and did not doubt the abilities of the women who were both young and strong as well. As they lay at anchor, bobbing in the chop, they needed no one at the wheel. But, when underway, Lonzo was occupied with the boat's operation. They would likely move against him as he slept or while at anchor. He had no weapon, while Lonzo had the Beretta. Searching Alta's purse in the dark revealed nothing of value, but the cutting board by the bedside laden with the antipasto yielded a knife. He secreted it away under his pillow on his side of the bed. Means, he had means once again, now to be patient while opportunity presented itself.

Williams feigned sleep and for many long painful minutes waited. Finally Alta returned to the cabin and quietly slipped in beside him while his nerve endings were alive with anticipation. As slow steady breathing signaled her sleep, he whispered to her quietly, then receiving no reply, placed one hand over her mouth and slit her throat.

For a single instant she tried to struggle, but then relaxed into the mattress, eyes wide. Williams dressed quietly, packing few clothes, then crept into the galley where a single bulb had made it possible to see one's way to the head. The door to the berth occupied by Lonzo and Leta was closed, with no lights apparent. Shoes in his jacket pockets, ditty bag over his shoulder, he moved barefoot across the deck.

Silently he pocketed some provisions, set two gallon jugs of water at the top of the ladder, and removed the stored supply of alcohol from its cabinet. Dispersing the liquid into the cushions and across the floor in front of the closed bedroom door, he lit the alcohol stove, pouring the remainder down the ladder as he exited topside. As a safety measure, he dogged the hatch from the outside just as the whoosh of the ignition sounded through the deck. Taking the small compass from the helm, he moved aft to the dingy trailing them on a line.

Williams could make out, first voices, then screams from below.

Reaching into a gear locker he found life jackets, rain gear, a signal pistol, first aid kit and small pieces of canvas and line. Smoke was coming up from below, but the screaming had stopped, as he, with his cache of supplies pushed away from the boat.

The water was calm, with a million stars overhead and a three-quarter moon giving him the only light. Now a mile distant, the boat burned and finally sunk without ceremony, taking its secrets with it. The dingy had no external propulsion, just a small tiller with which to steer. Williams realized it would be morning before he could see well enough to make plans which would take him to land, so he settled back against the gear bag and finally dozed off.

Hot sun in his face awoke him. During the night the swells had increased and the little boat, at their mercy, went from valley to crest as it chose. He had learned enough while taking the helm under Lonzo's instruction to know he must steer into the wave. He soon learned to operate the tiller with his free hand as he poured himself a short ration of water and indulged his hunger with salami and cheese. He guessed the boat to only be between 10'-12' in length, Williams distributed its cargo to make it ride more evenly while appraising its appointments.

The boat had two oars and two seats across its beam, one fore, the other aft. They were positioned allowing the occupant at the rear to reach the tiller while the other had a socket that allowed an oar to serve an impromptu mast. If fitted in this manner it was reminiscent of a sloop like those he had seen on the east coast.

Carefully Williams tied off the tiller with a short piece of line, allowing it slack enough to move slightly while keeping the boat heading into the waves, then he moved forward, fitting one oar into the socket. Next he checked the gear bag, finding several pieces of canvas. He chose one about four feet square and tied it to the remaining oar along its length, then tied that oar to the other, forming a cross. The two opposing corners also fitted with short lengths of line hung down and were run through the oar locks, then back to the rear. Returning to his seat, he could now adjust the angle of the sail relative to the beam of the boat thus catching the wind to his advantage.

Lastly, he removed the compass from the bag and found a place to mount it which was visible from his seat, he then pointed the bow northward. He elected a northwest course which kept him abreast of the waves. Knowing that they had sailed southward from Italy but with no idea of his actual location, he was content to be going toward land, be it Italy or elsewhere on the continent.

As the day wore on, he found it necessary to fashion a head covering for protection from the hot sun. The sea neither calmed nor increased, much to Williams' joy. He was well aware that neither the boat nor his skills were a match for the sea's fury. The breeze remained from the southeast allowing him to tie off the sail and just use the tiller for steerage. As the sun hit its apex at midday, Williams indulged in another ration of both food and water, judging the remaining supply to be sufficient for no more than three days.

As the sun set, the breeze eased and waves lessened, but no land was visible to him. His muscles had began to cramp from lack of movement and probably sufficient hydration, so he stretched out on the bottom of the boat, and lay on the gear bag to reduce his discomfort. A short line tied to the tiller and looped around his wrist gave him marginal control of the rudder but still sufficient under the current conditions. Presently he drifted off to sleep under the watchful eyes of the moon and stars.

The morning of the second day began in a panic. Water, driven by wind, slapped him in the face while around the boat six foot waves with white caps were breaking. As he regained his seat and assessed the situation, he was momentarily relieved to see the cause being the shallow water of the looming shoreline. But, just as quickly, his elation turned to dismay when no dock or civilization was apparent, the shoreline was an unfriendly looking array of rocks. He thought to strike the sail to slow his progress but quickly reasoned that without it's propulsion, he'd lose steerage and control.

In a more sophisticated craft with more experienced sailors it would have been possible to reduce the size of the sail while still retaining control, but he had no such option. He was doomed to hit the beach under full sail at whatever speed the wind chose. The most he could hope for was to steer between the rocks and to a friendly portion with sand or smaller rocks.

Williams, ever resourceful, carefully planned the oncoming encounter with the beach. Just prior to impact he stood, holding the gear bag in front of him as a shock absorber, he walked forward past the sail to the bow, having now abandoned the tiller completely. The beach ahead looked mostly sandy with small rocks and a backdrop of brush and small trees. With his weight forward, the small craft rode down by the bow, causing it to strike sooner, then rise as the waves raised the rear in their second effort. He was immediately pitched forward and out onto the sand.

With his weight gone, the bow then rose naturally and moved inland a full boat length in the current before coming to rest undamaged. Williams, however, was ejected at between 5 and 10 miles an hour hitting the ground hard, then rolling into the brush. Stunned, bruised, but unhurt, he was able to stand and then walk to the boat before grabbing it's lanyard and securing it to a small but hardy bush nearby.

With a sense of relief followed by elation, Williams wished he had thought to bring a bottle of wine to toast the event. He spent the early afternoon scouting the terrain in close proximity but hesitated to travel far afield with darkness threatening. After finding no sign of human activity, he returned and had little trouble starting a driftwood fire, then using the gear bag as a sleeping bag shell, with canvas and clothes to soften the ground, he enjoyed another meal before drifting off to sleep.

Tide, he had never had to deal with tide before, but this morning when he awakened he found the boat floating nearly beside the burned out campfire. He had been saved from getting wet by less than ten feet as the high tide broke nearby. Looking above, the day seemed to hold the possibility of rain. Low white clouds with dark grey bellies covered the visible sky.

As he slipped on his light windbreaker and his only change of clothes, he carefully laid out each piece of his belongings on the canvas bed, and took mental inventory. He then packed what was necessary for the day's planned exploration and wrapped the rest in canvas and buried it in the sand nearby.

He followed the coastline eastward until he finally came to a steep ravine which he used to travel inland without challenging the cliff fronts that faced the ocean. The cliffs surrounded a small fresh water stream that flowed from the mountains inland before dumping into the sea. He drank deeply, and then filled one of his gallon jugs, which was threatening to run dry, from a clear pool in the rocks.

Looking at the debris scattered nearby he guessed this stream would have made the ravine impassible at certain times of the year with its high flows. He walked without difficulty, slowly picking his way upward and enjoying the adventure. As the brush finally gave way to deciduous trees; birds, small squirrels, and mice announced his presence as he continued inland. Trails appeared, presumably made by larger animals, making his progress easier. Then suddenly, a crack of thunder exploded as the sky lit with shafts of lightning, followed immediately with plump warm droplets of rain. Thundershower, he thought, beginning to enjoy his communion with nature. As the tempo increased, Williams sought the shelter of overhanging trees, and then remembered the danger posed by the lightening and chose a rocky overhang instead. After 15 minutes the downpour had not abated but seemed rather to be increasing as he watched the stream beside him swell.

Williams had almost waited too long when a bell went off in his head and he realized the danger he was in. Flash flood, that seemed the logical next chapter in the book, and he was in the bottom of a ravine. Logic told him to seek high ground but also told him he lacked the time to get to the summit. He looked hopelessly at the steep rocky sides nearby that had given him shelter, but knew he had little chance to climb them.

Looking backward toward the distant sea, the vista was obscured by the falling rain, but he did consider that if he retraced his steps but maintained his current altitude he'd rise out of the valley and out of harm's way. So he turned back, side-hilling as he went along the valley wall. With each step the stream fell farther and farther beneath him as he angled toward the rim. He was going toward the sea but not losing altitude. Finally, muddy and wet to the skin, feeling secure a hundred feet above the torrent below, Williams stopped in a sheltered area. Shaking with cold and emotion he wondered at the possibility of hypothermia.

Unfortunately he had not packed the rain gear from the boat, nor had he a dry change of clothes. He had food, money, water, a knife, and the canvas bag. The bag, which he had used as a sleeping bag, was nearly four feet in length and made of heavy canvas. Fully clothed he slipped inside it, lying in a fetal position, it came up to his shoulders. He took time to tighten the drawstring across his chest, then lay on the dry earth and began to eat and drink his remaining provisions.

When Williams awoke, he was no longer shivering. He no longer felt cold except for his hands, and the rain had stopped. Overhead the cloud cover was breaking up and moving out to sea, but still sunshine scorned him. He could hear the roar of the raging water below him as it continued to grow independent of additional rain. It carried within its flow brush, small trees, rocks and debris from its last performance, all lethal to anything in its path. He was cramped, sore, and bruised but alive with a full stomach and the taste of yet another victory on his lips.

In another hour he was on the ridge, the western side of the ravine, and was walking up it toward the summit where he could see mountains joining together. He stopped frequently to catch his breath and drink deeply. He finally came to a plateau, then a traveled road, and finally could see human habitation in the distance. After evaluating his situation, he saw no reason to consider returning to the boat, what little he had buried could be replaced, with the possible exception of his passport. He wondered at the wisdom of using the Williams identity anyway with the possibility that his pursuers may still be looking for him.

He'd need to break the link to his employers, thus providing a dead end for both they and any law enforcement which may have taken up the chase. Lonzo had indicated that nearly everything you might need here in Europe could be had if you had money. He had expected to use Lonzo and his expertise to acquire them, but now he'd have to rely upon himself as he had done in America. He had a meager 5000

Euros in his possession, with the remainder in the safe at the hotel. How to extract those without leaving a trail indicating that he remained alive may be a problem. The million in his numbered account was, no doubt, off limits and almost certain to be monitored for activity. Ironically, he found himself a nearly broke millionaire.

His record now included ten kills, eleven with grandma, but his education was just beginning. Williams wondered if the Cameron Smith persona remained safe to use or if it had somehow been compromised also. Better safe than sorry he thought, both Smith and Williams were dead, leave them that way. In the hotel safe were three identities with credible documentation and sizeable bank accounts in the States that he had established without the involvement or knowledge of his employers. Somehow he would need to access the safe without bringing scrutiny upon himself.

He walked into a small rural village, not totally unnoticed but without fanfare, and entered a small café which boasted few patrons and a dismal atmosphere. He sat alone at the bar. After a few minutes the owner broke off his conversation with a local and approached him.

He laid some bills on the bar and ordered wine and cheese without difficulty, following the pattern his driver had drawn for him.

"Inglise?" he asked, asking if the tender spoke English.

"Not so much," answered the owner.

"Roma?" he asked hopefully.

From across the room came a loud reply in coarse but perfect English, "you mean Rome?"

"Yes," Williams replied. "I am looking to catch a ride there, how far is it?"

"About 35 kilometers, 20 miles or so. Are you in a hurry?" the man answered, rising from his seat.

"Not really," Williams replied, "but I lost my ride and luggage and need to find a way back."

"I can pay a little," he added.

The man had moved and took the stool next to him and eyed him openly, with a bit of arrogance in his walk. "How much?" was the question.

Williams had divided his remaining cash into two parts, one in his pocket and one in his shoe before coming into the bar. He played the dupe taking out a few crumpled bills while asking hopefully, "maybe 1,000 Euros?"

The man feigned irritation and answered too quickly, "3,000," obviously now into the game.

Williams knew he had a ride now and played along, pretending to count his bills, "1,500?" he responded hopefully.

"2,000 and a bottle", was the man's final offer.

"Done", said Williams, as he motioned to the bartender and paid for the bottle. Williams handed the bottle to his new chauffeur and rose from his seat. "Are you ready?" he asked confidently.

The man also rose, knowing now that he could have held out for more, as he ambled to the door behind Williams. The old green Peugeot that was parked near the front door started right up with a belch of blue smoke, then pulled away with them on board. On the trip into town they passed through one small village after another, coming finally to a paved highway. As they crested a small hill, the whole of the city spread out before them, huge and magnificent, like something from a history book. Rome was built both in mountains and valleys and it seemed to encompass everything in sight.

When the driver asked his destination he had already made the decision not to mention the hotel, but rather chose the café where he had eaten with Lonzo. As they pulled up in front he quickly exited, and handed his driver the agreed payment, thanked him, and walked right inside without further conversation. Hesitating a moment longer, the old Peugeot then pulled into traffic and was soon out of sight. When he appraised himself in the storefront glass his reflection was of a bum or vagrant, providing a disguise which had hardly been planned. He entered a nearby clothing shop, used the lav to do a cursory cleanup, and then chose a change of clothes. After paying the storekeeper, he carried the clothes with him rather than putting them on, thus maintaining his disguise.

Fearing the hotel may be under surveillance, he enjoyed a latté across the street as he watched the people coming and going. He saw nothing obvious but did notice that the hotel did have cameras, both inside and out. If he were to remain 'dead,' he would need to find a way to defeat the record of his visit.

It was early evening when he ate a light meal and then walked to a local theater where he could kill some time unobserved. At 1:00 a.m. the shifts changed at the hotel and the most junior of management employees occupied the front desk. He looked to be no older than 19 or 20, having probably gotten his job through a friend or relative already on the staff. The 'Manager' tag on his lapel gave him an ego lift in lieu of pay. As Williams entered, he had taken care to change into clothes which identified him as a valued guest.

As he approached the front desk, the pimple-faced 'manager' surprised him by calling him by name. "Oh, Mr. Williams, I am so happy to see you, we were worried when we had not seen or heard from you. Our cleaning staff discovered your room had been burglarized last night and we had feared for your safety."

"Yes, yes", responded Williams, "I fear that I am being pursued by cohorts hired by my ex-wife." As Williams spoke he laid a large flash wad of Euros on the counter. He had taken the time to wrap the remainder of his smaller bills in a €500 bill. The younger man's eyes automatically focused on the roll.

"I need a small favor", Williams said, keeping his hand on the roll. "I need to access my valuables in the safe and leave without any record of my return." He nodded to the cameras which were running. "I'll need to take the tape with me, and ask you to replace it with a fresh one".

"But sir," he began, "I could lose my job for changing the tape."

"You'll find it worth your efforts," responded Williams, "... and who but you and I will ever know?"

As he said this, his hand nonchalantly tapped the roll of bills on the counter, adding considerable emphasis. "But first, my valuables," Williams changed the subject abruptly while looking toward the hotel safe.

"Certainly sir" came the eager reply as he turned his attention to it, "just a moment."

So far so good, thought Williams, not a single patron had come or left during the exchange, they remained alone. William's plan B had included an ice pick in the ear of the younger man should he fail to buy into the first. He fingered the pointed instrument hidden in the sleeve of his jacket, hoping to not find it necessary, wanting to leave no new trail to be followed.

In a private area the size of a phone booth he was able to remove the entire contents of his box, noting with pleasure it was intact. Looking to his left he observed the young manager extract a VHS tape and replace it with another while not activating the camera. Williams accepted the offered tape, pressed the roll of bills into the eager hand, winked and said, "our own little secret, thank you." A short time later, from his table across the street, he noted the red light on the camera when it flickered on and began to record.

What next, he mused, where to go and what to do? The man who had never existed had died and remained lost at sea with his assassins. They, whoever "they" were, should have no way to trace him if he were careful. He checked into a small, out of the way hotel using his new identity, "Cleave Jamison," and went right to sleep after a hot shower.

His watch showed 10:00 when he finally roused, he felt refreshed after having paid his sleep debt in full. He wiped the steam from the small mirror after taking another painfully hot shower, but he chose not to shave. The four day beard aged him, rounded out his face, and gave him a haggard look. He toweled his hair dry but left it looking unkempt, wondering what persona would be most effective with a minimum of effort on his part.

Several thoughts had suddenly come to mind, a weapon, local passport and travel papers, an easily accessible bank account, and finally the professional training which had been offered in the Soldier of Fortune magazine. He wished he'd have pursued this while having Lonzo's help available, but unfortunately that opportunity was gone.

Williams/Jamison had no idea how to set up a numbered Swiss account, or if he should for that matter, but did know he could not carry around a half million dollars with him. He also questioned the prudence of leaving the three stateside accounts open longer than necessary, even under assumed names. He took a cab to a local bank and asked for a manager who spoke English.

When seated with the manager, he asked if there would be difficulty in transferring money from a stateside account to the local bank. He was assured there would be none if he could provide identification and the account number, he had both with him. Using his "Daniels" identification and passbook he asked that they transfer the entire $146,000 American to his new account. Explaining that he did not know the length of his stay in Europe he would find it more "convenient" to deal locally.

The manager, very impressed with his good fortune, bubbled over with enthusiasm and did some first class 'ass kissing.' When the transfer was verified and complete, the manager offered his new client lunch, at bank expense, in a small but very fine nearby restaurant. Mr. Daniels acted reluctant, but then accepted the offer with relish, after seeing his opportunity to glean needed information from the man.

Over a tasty lunch and several bottles of fine wine, the man talked incessantly in an effort to make himself seem important. Daniels listened, amused at the pompous ass, throwing in a pointed question now and then as the man rambled on. Where could one discreetly acquire a weapon for protection, where could one lease a more long term living accommodation, a local hair stylist, car rental, clothing, companionship, etc? The little requests were diverse and without pattern, keeping the man off base, answering questions without realizing it.

By his flush the manager looked to have allowed the bank to buy him a more than adequate amount of wine. When the luncheon came finally to a close, the manager offered to drop Mr. Daniels wherever he liked. Daniels chose the man's recommended haberdashery where he purchased first a money belt and then several items of clothing, selecting each carefully to fit the new persona that he was trying to create.

He was quick to drop the manager's name and while the man was still glowing in the praise offered, he asked him about the stylist? The shop owner concurred with the manager's assessment and pointed him to the shop just down the street, of course after accepting a large tip.

Daniels indicated to the stylist that he was going for the 40-plus "grunge look," wanting to remake himself in his new home, while indicating he may be coming off a bad marriage and going through a mid-life crisis.

They talked while she shampooed his hair, and answered his questions in passable English, she recommended that the transition would take several visits and another month while his hair grew out. She thought a dusting of grey would add to the look while the natural grey in his beard would confirm his maturity without further aging him. She indicated his hair, layered over his ears, would soften the angles of his face without making him seem fat.

He himself had decided to trade his clear contacts for ones of color, then possibly heavy framed non-prescription glasses to hide his eye structure. There was little doubt that 'they' had means to analyze photos as did the more sophisticated law enforcement agencies worldwide. He had watched his share of crime and drama shows to know that computer analysis would spot him in a minute where a human may not. Was it worth it? He had to ask himself, how far was he willing to go with the makeover? Was plastic surgery a viable option, what could be done about finger prints? Could he ever go home?

He had asked the stylist to dine with him but she had indicated previous commitments, so he dined alone before returning to the hotel. Looking back over his day, he was pleased with his accomplishments. He vowed to continue on his current course, carefully planning his transition until he felt secure. As he drifted off to sleep he thought of Lonzo's home and how peaceful the adjoining country had been. Perhaps he'd find a villa to lease somewhere out of the city.

That night he slept fitfully, reliving the details of the ten whom he had killed. At 2:00 a.m. he awoke, someone was standing over his bed holding the ice pick. A chill came over him when he realized he was out of bed looking down at where he himself had been lying.

Sleep never returned, finally at 4:00 a.m. he showered, dressed in his old dirty boat clothes, and took a cab after first asking the driver if he spoke English. Though not fluently, they understood each other well enough to communicate.

Daniels gave him a name which the banker had indicated as one who just might provide a weapon for a price without too many questions. They drove straight away to the side of town where fishing boats, warehouses, and dumpy bars frequented the streets, finally they pulled up in front of a storefront with a single light in the window. Daniels tore the fare in half indicating that the driver wait for his return, then knocked on the door.

Soon a voice asked through the locked door what he wanted, he simply said, "Vito". The door opened but he was not admitted as another light framed him against the night.

"Your business?" was the question asked.

"Pistola", was the one word answer from Daniels, as he was allowed inside. He could not clearly see who was doing the speaking in the darkened room, but sensed that more than one person was present. The light was reoriented so that it shone only on him, then strong hands searched him, removing his coat. Daniels was glad that he had resisted the urge to bring the ice pick which would surely have been found and taken as a threat. "Vito?" he repeated, supplying the banker's name and station.

After what seemed an eternity, a heavy voice asked, "what are you looking for?"

Daniels used the only information in his storehouse, "Beretta, Model 86, .380, and ammunition."

"For what purpose?" came the amused question. "Protection," Daniels answered.

"From who?" was the next question. Daniels had not been prepared for such interrogation and had no answer.

Finally he stuttered, "E... enemies".

"And how do you know that I am not your enemy?" Vito replied. "How do you know I will not just shoot you and take your money?"

Daniels shivered, he did not, and now wondered why he should expect a stranger not to rob and kill him.

Trying to sound braver than he felt, Daniels answered, "that would be bad for repeat business."

Vito laughed a hearty laugh, then motioned him to a seat. "Very true, no repeat customers."

Vito left the room, coming back with the Beretta and a box of ammo, "€1,500." Daniels had €2,000 in one pocket, more in another if needed. He counted out €1,500, then stood.

Vito smiled and asked, "anything more?"

"Maybe, yes, is there someone who can teach me the arts of survival?" Daniels asked.

"Call me tomorrow," said Vito, handing Daniels a scrap of paper with a phone number scrawled across it, "I'll ask around."

Daniels laid two more bills on the table and said simply, "Grazie."

The cabby was waiting where he had left him as he returned.

"You were gone a long time", he said, trying to sound perturbed, "it will cost more."

Daniels gave him the fare which had been torn in half and added €200 to it, smiling. It was taken without comment as the cab pulled away.

Half way back to the hotel, Daniels asked, "do you know the area in the hills nearby? I am thinking about maybe moving out of town for a while."

The answer came, "my sister lives to the north, and I to the north and east. It is a fine place to raise a family."

"Perhaps we could see the sights together, in the daylight," Daniels replied, "maybe tomorrow?"

The cab driver said, "alas, tomorrow is my day off, but I could drive you in my own car for a fee if you like."

"Yes, your name?" Daniels inquired.

"Louie," came the reply, "what time should I pick you up?"

"Around 10:00," answered Daniels. "First we have breakfast, then spend the day together. How much would you charge?"

"Is €600 too much for the day?" Louie asked tentatively.

"No, Louie that is fair, at 10:00 then," Daniels said as he left the cab, and walked to his room.

If Daniels thought the taxi was junk, Louie's car was worse. However it did start right up and ran smoothly. They did not seem to put much value in the appearance of their vehicles but must care for them mechanically, he thought to himself. He began the conversation with an offer to buy them breakfast. Louie did not reply, but rather just nodded and took them to a local café.

Daniels was pleased as he ate. The food was good, served in great quantity by a woman of huge dimensions with a friendly smile. It was obvious that she enjoyed food and life in general to the max. They spoke as they ate, Daniels found that Louie was from Napoli, had fathered four daughters and two sons, and lived with the only woman he had ever loved. He gave Daniels a picture of a hardworking man with a good grasp of who he was and what was important to him. Daniels envied him, wishing momentarily that his own life had been simpler.

Not obvious, but hanging heavily in the inside pocket of his light jacket, was his new friend, Mr. Beretta, its clip loaded and snapped into its butt.

Their first stop before leaving the city was his bank, where he secured a safety deposit box and emptied the majority of his cash from the money belt into it. He had now close to 250,000 Euros easily available, some in the new account and the remainder in the box. He would need to do something about the two remaining accounts in the U.S. but remained undecided just how he wanted to do that. He carried another €15,000 or so scattered about his person.

As they left Rome, traveling north, they ironically were traveling the same way as he had taken with Lonzo several days before. Louie became relaxed and took on the role of a tour guide, and pointed out items which he thought may interest his guest. They wound up the hill, finally passing the turn off that would have taken them on a dead end into Lonzo's driveway, until all of Rome could be seen far below with the ocean far in the distance. He guessed 30 miles, and then asked the driver how far to the sea. Louie shrugged then answered nonchalantly, "maybe 40 kilometers", 20 to 30 miles.

Soon the road forked, with the paved portion following the ridge while the other broke away to the east and crossed the valley. Here and there they passed homes, vineyards, and small farms with children, cows, and barking dogs. Louie pointed across the canyon indicating where his sister lived and motioned ahead where his family lived. Louie seemed genuinely pleased when Daniels asked if he could meet his family.

Daniels was quickly learning how to manipulate people simply by showing interest in what interested them. In this case, however, he had asked without motive, just out of curiosity, to know more about the

driver. When they pulled into the drive, a smallish whitewashed structure greeted them, followed by dogs barking, children running and
laughing, and a plump, dark haired woman with a broad smile, who
followed from the front door.

Louie greeted and hugged each child, then turned and swept his
bride from her feet, all the time talking incessantly in Italian. None of
the children spoke or understood English but that did not stop them
from talking with the stranger, a mile a minute.

Louie's eyes shone with love as he introduced his wife, who could
speak and understand a little English, but was obviously self-conscious
and uncomfortable with it. 'Cluttered' was a poor choice of words to
describe the inside of the house, 'lived in' seemed more appropriate to
Daniels. What little furniture they had was worn but clean, much of it
looking handmade. Wine, cheese, bread, and salami came from
nowhere as the wife chose their finest wineglasses for their guest, with
children crowding in a circle around the kitchen table behind the
adults. Daniels felt embarrassed at the special treatment and wondered
how often Louie entertained guests.

After they had eaten and visited, he and Louie walked the property
together, with the children and dogs following behind. Louie's wife
busied herself in the kitchen, already preparing to bake bread and cook
dinner. Louie pointed out the property lines, the buildings and their
use, and took particular pride is showing his shop to his guest. It was
here where he made furniture, later to be sold in the shops in Rome at
high prices.

It was obvious also that the shops kept most of the sale for themselves by his need to drive the cab to supplement their income. They
owned sheep, goats, chickens, and a single cow which furnished milk
to be made into cheese and butter. They seemed, to Daniels, to be very

happy and self-sufficient in their poverty. It was hard for him to understand happiness without money as he had never been introduced to the principle. He wondered for a moment if his parents had been happy working side by side in their little bakery.

He was seated first, like royalty, at the head of the table and served while eager eyes waited for him to pronounce his approval before they would begin to eat. The food was wonderful, Daniels smiled and nodded his approval, gesturing them to eat. They needed no further invitation and descended upon the table like locusts with rich hearty tomato sauce and pasta flying from plate to plate. Warm bread, butter, and cheese, were passed from hand to hand until each plate overflowed. Some kind of fruit pie was for dessert covered with thick cream.

The car angled down the rolling hillside taking them back toward town with Daniels feeling a kind of melancholy loneliness, missing the closeness which he had encountered at their home. He wondered if it were too late for him to pursue that kind of life, or if it were even real and not just a pretense. They traveled in silence for the most part, just making small talk, having lost the closeness that they had shared.

Once in Rome, Louie asked if there were other places he'd planned to go before returning to the hotel for the night. Taking a chance at hurting the man's pride, Daniels asked, "is there someplace where we could stop that I might be able to buy a thank you gift for your family for the wonderful day?"

"That is not necessary," Louie replied, sounding embarrassed, "we were just offering our friendship."

"Louie," Daniels said, looking him directly in the eyes, "I have no other way to thank you and show you my friendship. Money is a poor substitute I know, but it is all I have to offer you." Nothing was said for a while, but then as they pulled up at the hotel, Daniels pressed a large handful of bills into Louie's hand. "Thank you", he said.

This may have been the first time when Daniels had felt a true emotion. It both scared and pleased him. He wondered if he could ever return to his previous life.

That night he slept fitfully, visions of faces and places haunting his dreams. Faces of his victims taunting and cursing him, the face of Leta as she died, her eyes asking him why, and finally the smiling faces of Louie and his family encouraging him that there was still time to find peace.

He called Vito as promised, but hesitated, not knowing exactly how to begin, then said, "Sir, you asked me to call. Perhaps you have information for me?"

"Yes, I think I do, but we should discuss such things together over a glass of wine," replied the now familiar voice.

"That would be my pleasure," responded Daniels. "Could you recommend a place?"

He could almost see Vito smiling over the phone when the reply came, "Café Alana, in two hours," before the phone went dead.

Daniels called the hotel manager and asked about the café and was told it was nearby, very popular with the locals, serving a fine selection of wines and good food. Daniels, as he was known now by his banker, or Cleave Jamison at the front desk, elected to wear his new clothes. He checked the placement of his finances, distributing them in his wardrobe, and made the decision to leave his gun in his room.

He no longer felt the need to protect himself from Vito who could have easily killed him last night if he had wanted. He expected this to be a social evening among business acquaintances, nothing more.

Daniels arrived twenty minutes early, taking a seat near the rear, facing forward, his back to the wall. Vito entered with two others, both took a seat at a nearby table while Vito approached him as if he was an old friend. Daniels rose, automatically sticking out his hand. Vito ignored the hand and gave him a great bear hug and loud greeting. He could feel the larger man checking him over for weapons as they clung to each other.

They accepted a bottle of wine, Daniels allowed him to choose the vintage, then took menus from the server as if to dine. Vito casually slid a small paper with a name and number across the table toward Daniels saying, "I know nothing of him, a recommendation of a friend. One might do well to make further inquiry before going into business with him," he advised. "For a small fee, I could look over your shoulder when you meet."

"Thank you," said Daniels, "I would not even know whom to ask about him. I'll call you after I have set up a meeting. May I ask another favor? Could you recommend a shop where I can purchase the right kind of luggage for Mr. Beretta?"

Vito laughed a hearty laugh, "Mr. Beretta? Yes, I myself have just the proper luggage for him. I'll see that he gets it."

They finished the bottle and had another, ordered upon the recommendation of the server, and laughed as if they were old friends. Daniels had begun to like the Italians, their open friendliness and love of life. The few he had known since he had arrived had been very different, and yet shared a zest for life previously unknown to him.

When finally they stood to leave, Vito addressed him, "Mr. Daniels, or is it Mr. Jamison, I have very much enjoyed our time together, we should do it again."

Daniels was taken off guard by his manner and the way he had handled his phony names. He had never felt the need to mention any name in conversation while using Vito liberally. Lesson learned. Vito had taken time to look into his identity before offering his help and friendship.

"Please call me Roger," he said with some embarrassment, looking the man in the eye. Daniels wondered how much he really knew about him.

Daniels/Jamison remained in the hotel, not wanting to make a decision on more permanent housing until he would see how the survival training issue was resolved. The next day he made the call to the number given him by Vito. The phone was answered by an English speaking voice with a heavy German accent. Daniels stated that he was a freelance international courier who had come to question his own ability to survive in an increasing hostile world. He was looking to learn those skills from trained professional teachers, a friend had offered this number.

"Perhaps our organization could be of help, but we are very selective of our clientele, who did you say your friend was?" was the question asked.

"I did not," Daniels came back, "I too, am selective of whom I employ."

It must have been the right answer, for the man laughed and said, "very well, when can we meet to discuss the details?"

"Café Alana at 6:00 if that suits you, I'll be wearing a red shirt," answered Daniels.

"At 6:00 then," was the reply before the dial tone sounded. Daniels immediately called Vito and gave him the details and the meet was set.

Not desiring to establish a connection with his financial life, he became Cleave Jamison for the purposes of this meeting, going to the extent of making reservations under that alias. He was certain that he'd be checked up on and this name ran into a dead end at his hotel. He carried no ID or documentation with the name. When remembering his encounter in the alley with the Mexican drug dealer and his feeling of vulnerability, he pocketed Mr. Beretta before leaving early for the rendezvous. When he arrived he was relieved to find Vito and several friends already enjoying wine with dinner.

As he was shown to his table he found a gift wrapped box waiting for him. Curious and amused, he unwrapped it, then peeked inside but did not remove the contents. He smiled and raised his head catching Vito's gaze, then nodded imperceptibly in gratitude.

After a few minutes he ordered wine and excused himself to the lav with the gift. Locking the door behind him he took out Mr. Beretta's new luggage and adjusted it, not without difficulty, until it rode smoothly in his armpit. With his jacket on, there was no external sign of a weapon, but he, feeling its weight, bristled with confidence.

There was no mistaking the man as he entered, he breathed authority, walking not with a strut, but with an air of confidence born of ability. Perhaps a shade over six feet, he appeared to be early forties, with a muscular frame and dark hair. Cleave guessed an ex-soldier who had tired of being underpaid and fighting for losing causes while answering to lesser men. Cleave stood, looked him directly in the eye, offered his hand without emotion. "Jamison," he offered.

Curtly, the man replied, "Smith", taking the offered hand in a firm grasp. They stood for a few seconds appraising one another while their hands struggled for advantage. They then seated themselves opposite one another. Cleave, relieved that the encounter was over, offered wine which was accepted without ceremony. Smith asked as to the scope of the training desired while he continued to size up his subject. Cleave, who struggled not to show weakness in the face of this overbearing personality, answered each question without elaboration.

He could see that less was more when attempting to be something you were not, not wanting to be tripped up in a lie. He was vague when speaking of his employers and the details of his "courier services", wanting to give the impression of loyalty to their confidentiality.

"3000 Euros a day," was what Cleave heard, the number he had been wondering about, "When would you like to begin?" Smith asked.

"Where and how long?" countered Cleave.

"A small island near Malta, how long depends upon you," Smith said sarcastically. "Some learn faster than others. How will you pay?"

Cleave thought for a moment... cover your bases... "Cash, a week up front, then by the week until we are done."

"Two, up front," Smith insisted. "Some don't last the week."

"Agreed," Cleave said. "Here's my number, call me when you are ready."

"I have your number," was the whispered response, "We'll pick you up at your hotel in two days, have the cash with you." Cleave nodded, saying nothing as Smith rose and left the room.

He watched as Vito rose and walked to the lav, saying nothing as he passed, then waited several minutes before he followed. Cleave recounted the exchange in detail to the Italian who listened without interruption.

Finally Vito spoke, "I know of the place, a private island, and have heard of its reputation. Patrons arrive from all over the world. They stay a short time and leave."

Cleave felt relieved, but questioned, "any advice?"

"Don't make it more attractive to eliminate you than to train you. Rely upon their need for "satisfied customers" and "referrals" as your means to stay alive. Make it clear that you may be able to send others to them in the same way you were sent."

Cleave took his hand while pressing several thousand Euros into it, then simply said, "thank you my friend, Mr. Beretta said to thank you as well."

Vito laughed his hearty laugh and shook his head, then said, "tell Mr. Beretta hello!"

On the walk back to his hotel, Cleave marveled at his new life. Just a week ago he had left New York, lacking self-confidence and direction, at the mercy of his employers, with few skills to even exist in this foreign country. Now he was reminded that he was rapidly learning to be self-sufficient by the weight and bulk under his arm.

Back in his room he formulated a plan, knowing he'd need access to thousands of dollars over the next few weeks, but not wanting to carry that amount with him. The very next morning he met with his banker and set up a wire transfer in the amount of €21,000 per week. The transfer would be initiated from another location by the use of a predetermined code word. Daniels had a cover story that he would be traveling out of country that may not have bank access but would have phone connections.

He doubted that the banker believed the story but he had not questioned it. They enjoyed another lunch together, this time Daniels offered to buy. Well into their second bottle of wine a local news bulletin flashed across the flat screen at the bar. Daniels could not understand what they were saying but immediately recognized the old green Peugeot which had brought him to the city. Turning to his guest he inquired the nature of the bulletin. The banker, who had not paid attention until now, listened as they repeated the message and revealed that there had been a murder in a small village just outside of Rome where a man had been tortured, then killed, his body had been found in the burned out Peugeot.

Daniels felt the blood drain from his face, utterly certain that the dogs had picked up his scent and were now pursuing him. Without being obvious, he finished his glass, then made the banker aware that he had a pressing commitment which he must keep.

His mind was racing, Daniels questioned how they had picked up his trail, the life boat of course. He had intended to return to it and had not taken precaution to hide or destroy it. The identification of the survivor was made easy by his fingerprints, with its proximity to the village also an easy connection. With few English speaking visitors he had been easily identified, his chauffeur probably made the mistake of holding out information or demanding payment. Obvious to him now was that no expense would be spared to find and eliminate him. He made a decision which came with some regret; he must eliminate the night auditor who would spill his guts in a minute when pressed.

At 12:39 the young man appeared, walking down the deserted sidewalk toward the hotel where he worked. Daniels waited for him to pass by the street light and into the shadows beyond, then pulled the .380 and placed two between his shoulder blades. Although the sound seemed deafening to him, it was just a pop-pop to anyone a block or more away. Daniels picked up the spent shells then walked slowly down the side street while trying to remember other loose ends which he may have left.

He awakened early, enjoyed a nice breakfast, packed a few clothes, counted out €42000 into an envelope, and waited for his ride. He was startled when his phone rang, the caller said, "Jamison, this is Smith, your ride is on its way." He had no opportunity to respond before hearing a dial tone.

He, of course, had never 'gone away to camp' as a boy, but visualized how they must have felt the same butterflies as he, when doing so. Excitement and fear of the unknown, anticipation and dread, questions yet without answers filling his mind. He heard a car stop, door open and close, then a knock on the door. As he opened it, a man stepped quickly inside pushing him roughly backward, a silenced automatic in his hand. Expertly the man patted him down, withdrawing the Beretta from its hiding place.

Then shoving him onto the bed, he spoke, "Mr. Williams, you are a hard man to find and seem very resourceful also. I have been sent to tell you goodbye."

His smile, which had filled his face, became a death mask as another man had entered behind him, grabbed his head, and with a single motion snapped his neck.

As the first man crumpled to the floor, the second offered a thin smile. "Your ride is here, I hope you are ready to go."

The irony of the encounter had not escaped him. His assassin had been assassinated by one of his new "teachers". It had been quite a demonstration if one had reason to question their abilities. Jamison/Daniels/Williams knew immediately that he could never return to this hotel and would likely be blamed for the body in his room.

"What about him?" he asked his protector.

"What about him?" was the reply?

"If you plan to leave him, I'll need to take the rest of my belongings with me." Cleave explained.

"Then bring them, we have no time to dispose of the body properly," he answered. "They know you are alive anyway so he will serve as a warning to them."

Cleave re-holstered the Berretta, and grabbed the assassin's silenced gun, shoving it into his bags, made a quick trip around the room gathering what few things he owned, then followed his ride out the door. They did, however, take a few minutes to relocate the assassin's vehicle around the corner, parking it between a couple of other vehicles.

"Mr. Smith should have explained that we are only here to train you, not protect you or take sides in whatever issues that brought this man to your door," the driver explained. "That I was there at a time when intervention served both our interests was fortunate, but should not be relied upon once your training is complete. Do you have the required deposit with you?"

"Yes," Cleave answered, passing the envelope with the €42,000 to him.

They drove in silence for 20 minutes, leaving the outskirts of Rome and into an industrial area. Cleave could see the expanse of the water in the distance as they parked in the shadow of a large, darkened building, then proceeded on foot the last hundred meters to the waiting helicopter. He knew little about aircraft but could see this was of substantial size and appeared to be military in design, powered by two jet engines. Its rotors were turning, with marker lights flashing, as it awaited their arrival.

His driver passed the car keys to another who had left the craft, who then returned to the parked vehicle, as they boarded the chopper. Cleave was seated beside his driver, with only the pilot and co-pilot on board. The door shut, the engines gained momentum, the craft lifted off without ceremony before angling over warehouses, the shipyard, and finally the Mediterranean ocean.

They flew almost silently over the water at over a hundred miles an hour and less than a hundred feet above it. The day was clear and the water calm, an azure shade of blue as far as the eye could see, with only an occasional boat in the distance now and then. Cleave could not help wondering if their course took them near the grave of the sunken sailboat he had deserted less than a week before, as he strained his eyes to see evidence of it.

About an hour later, he could see one large and several smaller islands ahead, then turned to his driver and asked, "is that our destination?"

"The smaller one on the far left," was his reply. "The big one is Malta."

Cleave wondered if they had names, but chose not to ask, thinking his curiosity would not be rewarded or appreciated. If for some reason he needed to know later, he suspected that using the larger island as a "known," the smaller ones also would be identified on a map. They landed with hardly a noticeable bump in the center of a paved area, adjacent to a small hanger. Immediately the engines were shut down and the door opened revealing Smith, flanked by two others, all in military dress.

"Welcome Jamison," came the greeting with a half smirk, "it sounds as if our timing was fortunate."

Cleave, who refused to be drawn into a conversation concerning his 'employers' ignored the remark, saying only, "yes".

"Follow me," Smith ordered, leaving little doubt as to who was in charge, as he turned and headed toward a barracks, bracketed by two men carrying weapons. As Cleave fell in behind them, the driver brought up the rear, carrying his two bags.

Inside the barracks were four cots, two had gear on them, two did not. The driver threw Cleave's bag on one of the empty bunks before handing him the other.

"Get dressed," Smith instructed. "Stow your civvies in a locker with your weapons," he said, pointing to a row of lockers on the wall. "Then come outside."

The BDU's fit as perfectly as one could have expected, and gave him kind of a rush just wearing them. Jamison was printed on a piece of heavy cloth that was velcroed to his blouse.

The shoes, however, felt a shade too big until he put on the heavy military issue socks, which filled them out. Smith had been adept at sizing a man up in just the few minutes they had shared in the café. Cleave wondered at how deeply he had been able to look into his heart as well. When 'Jamison' exited the barracks, Smith and the driver were waiting for him.

"Jamison", he said, cutting right to the chase. "You are paying a lot of money to learn things which may very well save your life, there's no sense in wasting time." You'll do what we say, when we say it, without question, is that understood?"

There was a short pause before Jamison replied, "yes."

"No," said Smith firmly. "Not yes, but yes sir! Everyone here is better than you, smarter than you, and knows more than you, they each deserve your respect. 'Sir' shows your respect. Is that understood?"

This time Jamison did not hesitate, answering "yes sir!"

"Very good, now show me you can do 20 pushups," Smith ordered. Jamison soundlessly dropped to the ground and did 20 pushups, slowing only toward the end.

"You will undergo several areas of training by a specialist in each area. It will not be necessary for you to understand the "why" when asked to do things. Some things are for physical discipline, some for mental discipline, some are defensive while others offensive in nature. The physical regimen is to build strength, speed, and stamina, not muscle mass. You should look only slightly more fit when you leave than when you came, but let me assure you that you'll be a different man. This is your last chance to ask questions, do you have any?"

Thinking which to ask of the million which came to mind, Jamison said, "no sir."

"Good answer, Jamison. Now give me 20," said Smith. "Mr. Jones, he's all yours." Jamison dropped once more to the earth and repeated the routine.

Jones spoke in a quiet but commanding whisper that reminded Jamison of 'Dirty Harry'. "You'll be asked to do 20 pushups and no more, approximately every 30 minutes, every day. This builds both strength and stamina. The only time you'll not do them is in the pool, shower, or on the range. Do you understand?"

"Yes sir," Jamison answered.

"Do you swim?" Jones asked, then without waiting for an answer, "how well."

Jamison replied, "Pretty well, sir. I was on the college swim team."

"How long?" Jones asked. "Two years, sir," said the recruit.

"No stupid, how long can you swim?" Jones asked.

"Sir, is that important?" Jamison asked baffled.

"How long can you stay on top of the water? An hour, a day, or a week?" Jones countered. "It might be important if you are lost at sea."

"I'm sorry sir, I have only swum in competition during a race, not for endurance. I have no idea," Jamison said, the light coming on in his head. They were trying to see what raw material they had to work with.

"Any other sports?" Jones asked, working to keep the disdain from his voice.

"No sir, but I run." Jamison offered. "In marathons..."

"Well, now we are getting somewhere. Any good? asked the trainer, with a hint of admiration.

"My best is 5th, but my times were respectable," responded Jamison.

"Show me!" said Jones, gesturing around the perimeter of the asphalt. "Now!"

Jamison fell into his gait and began around the mile long edge of the field, noticing right away the weight of the boots and BDU's, which added 10 to 15 pounds to his weight. After four laps he was beginning to breathe heavy when Jones yelled at him to "give me 20". He dropped and found difficulty now in the last five of the twenty, but completed them anyway. He then resumed his laps.

At 12 Jamison was breathing heavy and wondering how much longer he could keep up the pace when Jones signaled him in, ordering another 20 pushups. Jamison, now nearly exhausted, made just 18 before crumpling to the ground.

"Jamison, you owe me two," said Jones. "Hit the shower."

Jamison's hands shook as he attempted to untie his boots. As he leaned on the wall in the shower and let the hot water beat on him, then gradually adjusting the temperature to cold, he could feel life returning to him. He toweled off, changed to clean underwear, and re-donned his BDU's.

Jones snapped at him the moment he exited the barracks, "I need 20 plus 2."

Jamison obediently hit the deck and began the task at hand, wishing he had remained in the barracks longer to regain his strength. From 18 on it was a struggle, with shaking arms trying to refuse his brain's orders. By sheer force of will he finally finished the 22, lying for a moment before rolling to one side then standing up. Jones did not respond verbally but showed satisfaction in his eyes of the accomplishment.

Abruptly Jones demanded, "What is a weapon?"

Jamison hesitated a moment, giving it thought before answering, "Sir, a weapon is something which can be used either offensively or defensively to inflict injury." He was secretly proud of his answer, having taken care to cover all bases without being too explicit.

Jones did not hesitate. "Name three weapons which you possess at this moment." Jamison again took time to consider his answer, now very into the game. "Sir, my hands, my feet, my mind," he responded confidently.

Jones nodded this time, "But, do you know how to use them?"

"No sir, that is why I am here, sir."

"Very good, Jamison, let's do some class work," Jones said as he used his open hand to deliver a stunning blow to Jamison's sternum, then sweeping his feet from under him with his boot. Jamison hit the ground gasping for air, seeing stars as his head hit the deck, and finding himself pinned down with a forearm across his throat.

"Surprise often makes the difference between life and death," Jones offered, and then continued, "you must be mentally prepared to strike first. Always, always be prepared to use deadly force or don't use force at all. Hesitation is weakness and weakness will kill you. When you face an adversary, you determine up front whether to fight or flee. If you decide to flee, strike quickly, gaining a momentary advantage and go far and fast. If you determine to fight, strike quickly, then finish what you have started, being willing to absorb injury and pain without considering retreat. If you are alive, you have not lost. If you quit, you have already lost and will likely die also."

Jones dropped quickly to the deck beside him, removing his arm from Jamison's neck. "There are several areas of weakness to remember, some obvious, some less obvious. Eyes, throat, heart, groin, knees, nose and others offer opportunity to disable and even kill an opponent.

A finger or thumb in the eyes will stop anyone, a sharp instrument will kill. A blow to the larynx may collapse the airway causing suffocation. An upward blow to the nose will break it, causing bleeding and the inability to breathe. The right kind of thrust will cause the bone to enter the brain causing death. A well placed fist or kick to the sternum will break the bone, causing disability or may stop the heart causing death. The groin or knees will disable the person, allowing you to flee or kill. The right blow to the back of the neck will break the connection of the brain stem causing death, as will one to the temple area of the head beside the eye socket. Tomorrow you will begin a little hand to hand training with Smith, the emphasis will be on technique."

Both men stood, Jamison had regained his composure, but now saw the instructor in a new light.

"Now give me 20," came the familiar order. Jamison did 20 with less difficulty than before, and then stood waiting for orders.

"Most evenings we will have night ops and continued training, consider this a night off. You are dismissed to your quarters, mess in 45 minutes," Jones offered, turning and walking away.

As Jamison entered the barracks he observed two men already there, sitting on their bunks, talking softly. They looked up uncertainly as he approached, then stood, both saying "Sir" out of habit, not knowing if he were an instructor.

"Jamison," he said, "just another student like you." Jamison noted the relief in their faces as they approached and identified themselves and Saran and Baker. As they talked, he found that the smaller man, Saran was from Lebanon and Baker originally London, England.

Both had arrived a day earlier and had spent the day with their instructor in much the same way as had Jamison. Their specific reasons for being there were not asked or offered. Both men looked as spent physically as he felt, but neither complained.

Jones stuck his head in the door, "chow," he said.

There was no reveille as would have been normal in a military boot camp, rather just a horn signaling the beginning of the day at 05:00 hours. The three had been joined by a fourth sometime during the night, leaving no empty bunks. The new recruit was a tall black man somewhere in his 40's, from the salt and pepper in his hair, appearing no stranger to military life. Jamison guessed he'd been in the service but now wanted to freelance and needed a tune-up or additional training. Although friendly enough, the new man, White, was a loner. He did not choose to open up to the others, only speaking when spoken to. The four showered, shaved, dressed and mustered outside at 05:30, where Smith and Jones were already waiting for them.

"You have 30 minutes to eat. You will then be taken by your individual instructors to your training station for the day," said Smith.

There were twenty men total in the mess hall, four tables of recruits and one of instructors. Jamison guessed that the other two groups were at a different stage than they in the training process. They had a more seasoned or less inquisitive look about them, as they ate quietly without conversation.

The food was hardy and in no short supply, each man had three eggs, two biscuits with gravy, ham, bacon and milk or coffee. They also received a brown bag which was to serve in lieu of lunch, to be taken with them in a rucksack to their training station. At 06:00 Smith stood signaling that they were finished and left the mess hall and waited outside for them to assemble. Jones addressed a group of four men who followed him away. Likewise, a second instructor took a second group, leaving Jamison's group and one other. Smith took Jamison and the three with him, while the last instructor, a muscular dark-haired Hispanic man took the last.

Smith walked confidently ahead of them into the fringe of tropical forest which ringed the compound, following no visible trail, with Jamison second, the others following. Without warning, Jamison found himself with a bloody nose and both eyes watering as a branch whipped past Smith and caught him full in the face. Anger swelling up on him, he wisely stifled a shout, realizing that he was not a guest on a dude ranch to be coddled. Quickly regaining his composure he fell back into step, adopting a new vigilance.

As they came to a clearing the four hesitated, seeing no sign of Smith. Without a sound, Smith grabbed Saran from behind, placing his hand over the smaller man's mouth and pulled him backward. Smith put a finger to his lips signaling that Saran should be silent, and then moved forward doing the same to Baker. Smith then fell into step directly behind the taller man as White withdrew a knife from his boot, moving forward behind Jamison.

As White lifted the blade to plunge it into Jamison, Smith grabbed his wrist from behind, using its own momentum to drive the knife into his throat. White made a wet gurgling sound as blood filled his lungs, then dropped to the earth with the tip of the blade visible through the back of his neck. Jamison turned just in time to see Smith release White's lifeless body, unknowing of the fate he had been spared. Saran and Baker suddenly came to life moving forward, talking at the same time to Jamison.

"He was going to kill you!" they exclaimed with excited voices.

Dispassionately, Smith said, "First lesson, never trust anyone, never assume anyone is who they appear to be. Trust your instincts and always cover your back.

"It appears," he continued, "that Mr. Jamison has enemies who know he is our guest. The late Mr. White must have been hired to interrupt our training, but instead provided a valuable lesson."

"As you'll continue to see, there is a lesson to be learned in everything. Now, each of you replay in your minds the events of the last 60 seconds, asking yourselves how you could have acted differently, how you allowed me to get behind you, and how things would have turned out if I had been the enemy."

Jamison recounted the events of the previous day in his mind, trying to figure how his enemies had known were he had gone. White must have been with the intended assassin. He likely observed when they relocated his vehicle and then followed them to the helipad. That would account for him arriving late, needing to identify his trainers, and then arranging to join them. In hindsight, he now remembered thinking that White had an air about him, Smith had noticed it and prepared for it, he had also, but had dismissed it as unimportant, nearly costing him his life.

Turning to Smith, he asked, "Sir, where did you hide while we passed?"

"In plain sight, Jamison, always hide in plain sight," answered their leader. "I was one of those three trees back there you walked right by."

He added, "all of you learn right now, this is no classroom exercise, this is your life, treat it with the respect due it. This course is pass or fail, you pass - you live, you fail - you often die."

Next, Smith taught them to walk, moving with both speed and grace, placing each foot in the proper place, without making a sound. He showed them how to leave a trail without being obvious, when it served their interest and how not to leave one when not wanting to be followed. Each man in turn was chosen to be the "pursued" while the others gave him a head start, then tracked him.

Smith pointed out both the strengths and weaknesses he noted as they continued the exercise. It was nearly midday when Smith seemed satisfied with their progress and allowed them to break for lunch. Smith remained silent, keeping his distance from them, only answering when spoken to. The three relived the encounter with White and chatted about their experiences to date like school boys.

Jamison looked over just in time to see a red dot on Baker's chest before it was replaced by the red splash of a paintball. Before he could respond, a like yellow one took Saran in the side of the head at the hair line, pitching him forward. Jamison ducked instinctively, turning in the direction of the fire, seeing several forms materialize from cover, before being struck first in the shoulder and then in the head. He must have lost consciousness momentarily from the impact because he found himself looking up into Smith's face.

Joining Smith was Jones and his four recruits, who were several days ahead of them in their training, each carrying a paint ball gun. Their mission had been to track Smith's group and put them down, which they had effectively done. Smith's group of three had failed to listen when he had tried to impress the need to treat their training seriously, lapsing back into their comfort zone. They were reminded by the bruising and pain caused by the paint balls and the laughter of their attackers.

Smith and Jones had retreated a few feet and were conferring in low tones, presumably discussing the absence of Mr. White who had been left where he had fallen. Jones' group, who had come upon the body without explanation, had chosen to complete their assignment. One of Jones' men had been posted lookout at each end of the clearing at his instruction, the remaining two stood by with self-satisfied looks while Baker, Saran, and Jamison got to their feet and attempted to clean the paint off their BDU's.

Smith took control, barking orders to the entire group. "Double time back to your barracks. Mr. Jones and I will join you directly and discuss this operation in some detail. Dismissed!"

Smith's group let the more senior men take the lead, dropping in behind them, while another of Jones' party brought up the rear. Double time turned out to be a fast jog which Jamison ordinarily would have had no trouble maintaining, but with his throbbing head, he struggled. Saran also had difficulty keeping up, losing his balance and falling several times. When they arrived at the barracks they had 45 minutes to rest and get themselves together before being herded into a conference hall kind of building nearby, where Smith and Jones awaited them.

Mr. Smith spoke first. "Mr. White was apparently an uninvited guest, an insurgent, sent by unknowns to infiltrate and do harm within our community. He made the mistake of underestimating both our ability and commitment to the safety of our guests. We take pride in our operation and will take whatever action we deem necessary to maintain our reputation. Mr. Jones, would you like to debrief your troops?"

Jones stood looking each man squarely in the eye, then addressed them. "Men, you have just completed day three with some success. I am here to not applaud you but to correct your shortcomings. First and foremost, you were not to have taken head shots, which two of you elected. They could have caused serious injury to the new recruits, defeating the purpose of the exercise. In this family we do not show our prowess by injuring a brother upon whom we may come later to depend. Tomorrow you'll meet at the range for small arms training with live ammo. I don't expect to have to remind you to build upon what you have already learned to continue your education."

Smith stood, looking intently at his three, and then addressed them. "You have let me and yourselves down twice in a single day. Both times you could have easily been killed, how do you feel about that?"

He then continued without waiting for a reply. "Tomorrow you'll do better. Dismissed."

Jamison, Baker and Saran returned to their barracks without discussion, each replaying the events of the day over and over in their heads, each vowing privately to 'do better'.

Following the evening meal, as they left the mess hall, Smith turned to them once again, "I'll need 20 before I tuck you in." They dropped to the deck and gave him their due, then proceeded to the barracks where they showered and hit the rack.

It seemed just a few minutes later when Jamison was shaken awake. Smith leaned over him whispering, "the C.O. wants a word with you."

Jamison followed in Smith's footsteps across the pavement to the far side of the landing field without speaking. The full moon, which shone overhead, revealed a smallish building standing off by itself, lighted outside with a single dim bulb. As they entered, Jamison was amazed at the opulence of its interior. The room, only eighteen feet square, was almost a museum of fine quality tapestries, statues, guns, and memorabilia. Heavy, over-stuffed furniture, bordered by bookcases full of leather-bound books filled the room. On the opposing wall were pictures of military battles and shadow boxes filled with medals.

"Sir," said Smith, saluting. "Mr. Smith", the man replied as he returned the salute.

"Mr. Jamison, I am Colonel Brandt, I need to ask you a few important questions, please have a seat." Jamison sat as requested without speaking.

"Mr. Jamison, it seems you have made powerful enemies with a long reach. We need to know what we are dealing with here, so we may evaluate our future relationship and commitment to each other," said the Colonel in an even tone. "Please enlighten us."

"Sir," began Jamison weakly, not knowing how much he should share, "I truly am not certain."

"Come now Mr. Jamison, you know very well whom you believe wishes you dead and has the resources to follow you around the world. I expect you to be very candid with me right now or give me reason not to finish for them what they attempted," came Brandt's reply in a firm voice. "Mr. Smith has protected you to date out of dedication to your welfare as a client, but he is not your personal bodyguard."

Jamison flinched, sneaking a glance at Smith who nodded slightly in affirmation. Jamison began with his recruitment. He then described the victims, while not including the details used in their deaths.

He was not going to reveal the incident on the boat until the Colonel came right out and asked, "and the three on the boat with you?"

Jamison could see that the Colonel also had a long reach, with resources to gather information. "I believe they were employed by my former employers to eliminate me as a possible embarrassing leak," Jamison answered honestly.

"Now we're getting somewhere," Brandt said and then continued, "I agree. You worked your way up the ladder to the originally intended target, and then became a liability to them when the heat was turned up by their opposition. Question is now, who are "they", how do we de-escalate the situation and what should our involvement be?"

"You should note that we are a for-profit business, not the protector of the weak or righter of wrongs. What do you expect to offer which would encourage us to support your position?" he asked.

Jamison thought for a moment before answering, "I have a million dollars in a Swiss account but am quite certain that it is being monitored."

"You have my interest, go on," offered the Colonel.

"I purposely have not tried to access it, wanting to stay undercover, but obviously that did not work," said Jamison, thinking as he spoke again. "I am willing to commit half of it to you now, if you will help me."

Brandt did not immediately respond, but rather took a cell phone from Smith and shoved it across the table to Jamison. On its screen was a picture taken of him while he was unconscious in the clearing following the paint ball attack. He looked quite dead, the blood from his nose having ran down his face from the branch incident, the bruising of the tissue from the blow darkening his skin, and the red of the paint in his hair and scalp looking suspiciously like blood. The Colonel pushed a button showing a second picture, that of Mr. White lying in a shallow grave waiting to be buried with the knife still sticking in his Adam's apple.

"At this point they are awaiting word from their operative," mused the Colonel aloud, turning to Smith. "What if we texted them the picture of Mr. Jamison as though from Mr. White, indicating the operation was successful, then wait a time and send the second picture, advising them that we do not appreciate uninvited guests on our island?"

"Of course," he continued, "we'll have to initiate the wire transfer before Jamison appears dead or they will see through the ruse."

"Mr. Jamison, are you prepared to get the ball rolling?" he asked.

"Yes sir!" was his immediate reply, "though I know little of how to initiate such things."

Colonel Brandt smiled and answered, "I'm sure we can facilitate it for you from this very office."

As they entered the adjoining office together, Jamison was

impressed. The room was full of electronics, radios, phones and computer screens of all descriptions.

"Sir?" asked Jamison, "may I ask you a question?"

"Certainly, ask away," responded the Colonel as he seated himself in front of the computer.

"Sir, have you the assets to find out who the enemy is?" queried Jamison.

"Yes, though they seem to have the full use of the U.S. government's Intel community at their command. My thought is that we begin with who benefits from the deaths, who is in a position of authority to dupe the CIA, NSA, and FBI into being used, then narrow down our search to those few individuals", said the Colonel.

"And then?" asked Mr. Smith, who had remained silent throughout the interview.

"And then we deal with the threat the way we deal with any threat, Mr. Smith, quickly and permanently," advised his superior.

"Please join me, Mr. Jamison," Brandt offered. What is the name of your bank?" Jamison told him and watched as he moved through layer after layer of computer screens, finally coming to one which asked "access code."

"Your turn," invited the Colonel, giving up his seat. Jamison typed in seven numbers, then was given another screen to type seven more, which he had committed to memory. It worked just like his local bank but with a more complicated PIN. The system then asked for instruction, he chose electronic transfer, meeting the eyes of the Colonel who nodded, then was asked the amount to be transferred, which he entered, and finally the account number to transfer to. The Colonel regained his seat and surreptitiously typed in the required account number.

"Now Mr. Jamison, we kill you off," the Colonel said smiling. "Mr. Smith, would you do the honors?"

"Certainly sir came the immediate reply, as Smith opened White's phone and sent the picture with a short text message. "He's dead."

Jamison, who for the past several seconds had held his breath, exhaled trying to look nonchalant. Although in a "dark" business, these were men of honor and that honor had preserved his life once more.

Both he and Smith returned to the barracks, then parted ways. Jamison hit his rack but was unable to sleep. When he finally fell asleep, it seemed a moment later came the horn signaling morning had arrived. At 05:00 the barracks came alive, each showered, dressed in clean BDU's, and mustered outside where they were promptly asked for 20. Smith then led them to the mess hall where they ate and mustered again outside at 06:00 for instruction. Jamison noted that the three other teams were also assembled with their instructors.

Once again Smith addressed the whole assembly, advising that the three squads who had small arms training were to carry weapons as they continued their training. Each squad was given a color coded lapel pin approximately an inch in diameter that would identify them as "friendlies" and their squad. He further explained that their security had been breached and deadly force was to be used against intruders. Introduced also were 15 additional members of the staff that had not previously been apparent, including Colonel Brandt. They too wore the same colored discs as did the instructors, bringing the total to five colors.

Jones took over their instruction at the range while Smith took the other group to a more advanced training. Smith was expert in demolitions, larger ordinance, booby traps, and improvisation. Jamison and his group became familiar with the AR15, M14 and 16, Uzi, Mac10, and two common Russians, being allowed to shoot each and ask questions.

They were not trained to be expert marksmen but rather to be able to pick up a weapon of opportunity and use it effectively. They were encouraged to become proficient, in their own time, with their weapons of choice through continued practice. They then fired the 45ACP until all cut paper with every round in their clip. Jamison found both Baker and Saran had a working knowledge of almost every weapon and possessed considerable skill in their use. He was grateful that Lonzo had taken time to show him the basics of the Beretta, keeping him from looking too foolish before his peers.

After lunch they were instructed in ballistics, the pros and cons of speed, bullet mass, the character of each bullet, and the need to choose either volume or accuracy in particular situations. Just before quitting they were issued paint ball guns and paired up, Jamison and Baker against Jones and Saran, in combat situations. After each encounter Jones would explain their errors and the obvious remedy to each. Finally, following another 20, they returned to the mess hall and then to their barracks. Jamison was exhausted, he elected to immediately shower and hit the rack.

The sound of the horn came unexpectedly, his wrist watch showed 02:15. Looking out, the field was completely lighted with massive Klieg lights, showing armed forms moving across it. Jamison's unit had not as yet been armed, but he remembered the Beretta and assassin's semi-auto in his locker. He donned his shoulder rig and armed himself, offering the second to Saran who was next to be dressed. Outside he could hear small arms fire being exchanged, shouts and orders being given.

Smith arrived simply saying, "We are under attack, Jamison, remain inside." There was no time to object as the other three left, Baker shouldering an offered M14. Jamison, feeling inadequate and unappreciated, finally came to the realization that men were risking their lives to keep his presence from being known. The exchange lasted only 20 minutes and left three insurgents dead, several wounded, one of the island's crew dead and three wounded.

The Spanish-looking team leader whom Jamison had seen but not met was seriously wounded as were two of the guests, another had been killed in hand to hand by a knife thrust from a more skilled combatant. Overall, the skill level on the island had been amazing considering the quality of their opposing force. None of the three left behind had identification or wore dog tags, but fit the description of Rangers, SEALS, or CIA black-ops by their dress and body builds. Apparently Brandt had anticipated the attack and had his teams at the ready when it all broke loose, saving the base from being overrun.

At first light the horn once again woke the camp. Leaders called their troops to muster where they were briefed by Brandt about the night's activities. He commended both the trainers and their recruits and gave a narrative of the overall battle. All but Jamison had been active participants, but lacked the overview of the whole operation. This report had the effect of bonding the teams together and giving them a lesson in the value of acting in concert and not independently of one another. Brandt said he believed that the attack would not be repeated but they were to stay armed and vigilant as they continued their training.

At mess, Jamison asked Smith in more detail about why he was not allowed to participate, but received only single sentence, "You're dead, remember?"

This made it clear to him they believed the attack was to affirm to someone if he was alive or dead. If the attack had caught them unaware, not only he but also many in the camp would have also been killed.

Training proceeded routinely throughout the next week, teaching new skills and honing ones learned earlier. At the end of Jamison's third week, nearly half of the early recruits had graduated and returned home, while a few new ones had arrived to begin training. Jamison was learning in the classroom, then applying what he had learned to field exercises in demolition, surveillance, communications, camouflage, improvisation, chemistry, and advanced hand to hand combat techniques.

By the end of the month he was playing cat and mouse with the instructors in the jungle, without direct oversight, using light charge explosives and non-lethal weapons against them. When Colonel Brandt called him in for an eval, all three instructors gave him critical ratings in the 90's and complemented him on his above average ability to adapt.

Brandt, together with Jamison, Smith, and Jones met later to discuss Jamison's former employers. Brandt said, "we do have some intel which points toward high ranking liberals in both parties. Most suspect to be coordinating the group is the President's own Chief of Staff, William Barker, who has connections all over Washington. Sympathetic cronies in the CIA, NSA, and FBI or others duped into providing assistance for "reasons of national security" have you in their sights, Gerhard Schmidt."

Jamison was taken aback, nowhere had he used his father's name in any of his dealings. The last record of Gerhard Schmidt was when he was in college after living with his grandmother.

"So, where do we go from here?" was Jamison's inquiry. "It seems hopeless."

"That, of course, depends upon you," replied the Colonel, "and your commitment. Do you want to take them down, or hide out until they find you?"

Jamison was incredulous. "Can I... we... do that?"

"Yes, I think so. Mr. Barker may have overplayed his hand when involving so many departments under the guise of finding a killer. A thinking man might question why so many resources were employed to find just one fugitive. Even a high profile prospective candidate like Mr. Dane doesn't have the stature to warrant a worldwide man hunt."

"Mr. Barker also has enemies. We begin by alerting them and planting the question in their minds as to why Mr. Dane's opponents would be so eager to find his killer. Get them to wondering why he has taken such an interest," offered the Colonel.

"As quick as they feel the pressure, Barker's cronies will begin to withdraw their support, fearing for their own careers. He'll be left out on the limb, all alone and vulnerable."

Jamison could see the logic, for the first time he began to hope.

The Colonel continued. "We have a friend in Greece who is a skilled surgeon, he will make computer matching of your eye structure very difficult and may supply you with new fingerprints as well, cadaver grafting, he calls it."

"If you are ready, you'll fly out in the morning," he added, "complete healing will take nearly a month."

Jamison nodded in affirmation. As they left the Colonel's office, Jamison felt at liberty to question Smith, "will you be among those accompanying me to the U.S. when the time is right?"

Smith hesitated, and then answered. "It would be my pleasure, Mr. Jamison, the man who was killed was a friend of mine."

Jamison had just left the cook shack when the rotors of the large chopper became audible. He quickly crossed to the barracks and gathered his rucksack, just as Smith entered saying, "better take it all with you, you may fly direct when the time comes to leave."

Jamison emptied his locker, then turned, sticking out his hand. "Thank you... thank you for everything." Smith took the offered hand, inclining his head slightly, but said nothing.

An hour and forty minutes later they touched down with a car and driver waiting for them. Jamison attempted conversation but found the driver either unable or unwilling to speak English. Approximately 30 minutes later they pulled through a gate and into a courtyard of an estate dating back hundreds, possibly thousands of years. Jamison noted that the gate was closed behind them by an armed guard. He was ushered inside by the driver who passed his bags to the waiting domestic in the foyer, who addressed him by name in broken English. Jamison was shown to his room where his bags were deposited before being shown into a great hall where his host awaited him.

The doctor introduced himself with a name longer than a wagon track, and then said, "my friends call me Cosmo." Jamison took his hand and nodded.

The man was squat and heavily built, like a wrestler or weight lifter, his hair black, flecked with a sprinkling of grey, his eyes dark behind rimless glasses, Jamison guessed him a shade over 50. He was jovial and direct when he came right up to Jamison and carefully looked at the canvas which was to be his masterpiece, touching Jamison's face here and there, while making comments to himself.

Uneasy, Jamison finally spoke. "Can you do it?" was the foolish question.

Cosmo smiled. "Yes, of course, the question of the technique which will give the best result is the consideration. Would you like a drink?"

Jamison took the offered snifter from his host, thanking him, asking, "when would you start?"

"Tomorrow, I think, or the next day possibly, whenever opportunity provides your new fingerprints. There are considerations you know," the doctor said quietly. "Pigment color, facial bone structure, age, and compatibility. If you are to "become" him, it is helpful that you share some basic similarities in the beginning."

Jamison froze. His donor was alive and was specifically being chosen for him. They were not going to just alter him, they were going to give him a new life with a history to go along with it.

Two days later an ambulance arrived at dusk, unburdening itself onto a waiting gurney that was wheeled into a side door on the ground floor. Cosmo had busied himself previously taking many, many pictures of Jamison, from every angle and position. Now he displayed each on a lighted board at the head of the operating table while glancing back and forth from them to the subject.

The man had been drugged and lay in a comatose state, being nourished by an IV. A little over an hour later Cosmo knocked and entered Jamison's room without invitation, holding several photos for his inspection. Jamison shuddered but maintained his posture as he looked at the man whom he was to become.

"Does it please you?" asked Cosmo proudly.

Speechless for a moment, he did not know how to answer, if he said yes, the man would certainly die, if no, they would begin to look elsewhere and someone else would die. Cosmo treated him like he was buying a used car and being shown a popular model.

The man, a Caucasian in his mid-forties, actually resembled Jamison; his coloring, skin tone, and hair color were much the same. The dossier indicated he was born in Germany but had been raised in England, single, age 42, previously an insurance salesman for Lloyd's of London, currently unemployed. It was unlikely he would be missed to the point of concern.

Assuming an identity has its benefits. Valid passports and documents necessary for travel, work history, travel history, and background information was already easily supported in many venues. It was far superior to inventing someone and trying to cover all the bases where an investigation might look. Of course one had to be careful to choose someone without bad affiliations and past history. Jamison asked if they had done a background check on the man and was told "yes" but only a cursory one. "We will do an in-depth one before surgery begins tomorrow."

Jamison took a deep breath, recalling the events of the last thirty days since he had arrived from America, he was overwhelmed. He also began to anticipate what his future may hold and began to look forward to the next chapter in his life.

Williams' information was known to every government agency including Interpol and TSA, in an attempt to eliminate the threat to his previous employers. Of course the charges brought against him had been broadened to include domestic terrorism as well as murder, so as to include the long arm of the Homeland Security who was not limited by the Constitution to the same degree as other law enforcement. In the electronic eaves-dropping ear, cameras worldwide would evaluate every photo and within a few minutes could computer match it to any known threat. If he were to remain dead, he could not be allowed to be seen prior to the surgery and his recovery.

Warren Barker had become consumed with the pursuit and elimination of Gerhard Schmidt, alias Roger Williams, to the point that most of his day involved checking in with his sources. While he would have liked to have believed the photo of the dead man was real, he was uncomfortable with accepting it in the same way he had been reluctant to believe Williams had gone down with Lonzo in the sailboat. That skepticism had borne fruit but had not given him a corpse to finger-print and DNA test. The stakes were too high to assume anything.

Colonel Brandt and his network continued to work covertly, unknown to any but his two trusted team leaders and Mr. Williams/ Jamison/Schmidt. Innuendoes had been planted subtly in the right places, causing some to begin to question certain activities within the Intel community. Little by little Barker's enemies began the process, as the Colonel had hoped, to look into the reasons for his interest in some-thing far removed from his regular duties.

A particular 'bull dog' journalist, unsympathetic to the current administration, had been given the loose end of a string, causing him to compare the similarities of certain recent deaths. His contact in the local P.D. had been a close friend of a couple whose murder investiga-tion had hit a dead end, but now felt a recommitment to it. As the plan moved forward, Brand's contacts stateside dropped a breadcrumb from time to time, leading them in the desired direction.

It was not necessary to make Mr. Jamison an exact duplicate of the donor, but just to enhance their similarities while downplaying their differences. In the end, Jamison had only to resemble the credible documents which he carried, while allowing the fingerprints to dispel any suspicion. When he awakened, he was told that his surgery took only three hours and the donor's another two.

Jamison was on his feet the next day but still well bandaged, both on the face and hands. His pain was controlled by medication and activities limited to reading or watching television while he healed. Cosmo would inspect his work each day, making comments to himself before reapplying new dressings. At the end of the first week, nearly all of the facial bandages had been removed and Jamison/Schmidt was allowed to see his face. He found it very interesting that looking in the mirror he had to look hard to see the differences until shown his 'before' pictures. One might compare the subtle nuances with having had a relaxing vacation and good night's sleep to being under stress and staying up late. When shown the donor's pictures vs. his mug in the mirror, he was amazed at the similarities. His fingers were still very tender and showed more result from the surgery than did his face.

Cosmo worked daily with each finger, using creams and anti-bacterial to facilitate their healing, assuring an invisible skin graft. Likewise the donor, who still was in an induced coma, was being given duplicate treatment unknown to Jamison. He was reticent to ask about him, fearing the expected answer.

After three weeks, only a pink coloration at the tip of each finger remained to testify of the surgery. Cosmo warned him of failure if his hands had hard use or were placed in water for an extended period in the next several months. Remaining inside still, Jamison became restless but used the time to study all the available information given him about his donor.

Conrad Schroeder had never been married, was orphaned at age five, had lived in England with a maternal aunt until her death, then was put into an orphan's home where he stayed until age 18. He worked at menial jobs while attending university, then was hired as an actuary at age 29, already having shown some ability with abstract numbers. No reason for his termination was given. He had remained unemployed for two years prior to visiting Greece, on his way to Switzerland to apply for a position with Zurich Insurance and Investments.

Schmidt/Schroeder liked that the man's heritage, like his, was German, encouraging him to try and remember his parents and what few words of German he knew. From Cosmo's library he was allowed use of an English-German dictionary and the use of a computer that assisted him in both language and German history.

Colonel Brandt arrived alone, and spent time with Cosmo privately before greeting the new Mr. Conrad Schroeder. With a bemused smile, the Colonel was shown into the library where Conrad had been working on the computer. "Mr. Schroeder," the Colonel greeted him, "we have some business to discuss."

As they spoke, Brandt updated him on the progress being made in America, and then turned to the subject of money. "It appears that you have used up your deposit, we are going to need additional funds to complete our mission. But first, let me bring you up to speed on our plan to guarantee that you are never pursued again. Downstairs, Mr. Cosmo has been the gracious host to the original Mr. Schroeder who has undergone the "reverse" of your own surgery. He now looks much as you formerly looked and proudly wears your fingerprints. He remains sedated but healthy."

"While the jungle photo has held them off for a while, we never did expect it to convince them of your untimely death, and since we must now access the remaining Swiss funds they will be aware it was a hoax," he continued. "Following that, our plan involves using your namesake to withdraw your remaining funds from your account in Rome, then with many witnesses in attendance;, he will be shot and killed as a victim in a robbery. Known to the bank manager and others as Mr. Daniels, but identified by his fingerprints as Roger Williams, his body will be cremated and buried by the government, leaving no reason for further scrutiny."

"How will you 'encourage' our victim to play along with the bank withdrawal?" asked the new Conrad.

"He'll awake thinking he had been the victim of a mugging and has been in the hospital for some time. We anticipate little trouble giving him a post-hypnotic suggestion while under chemical induced amnesia, planting a new identity as Daniels in his subconscious. He'll have your identification, your picture, your passbook and a dependency upon his care givers to help him recreate his past. He'll be immediately recognized and welcomed by the bank manager prior to the withdrawal," said the Colonel. "I see no downside, closing out your account will give you needed traveling money, stop the search for you, and allow your new identity to be more easily accepted."

Conrad was impressed. "May I ask you another question, sir?"

"Yes, certainly," came the immediate reply.

"I feel you have gone above and beyond for me, is this usual treatment for your guests?" queried Conrad.

Brandt laughed aloud, then replied, "hardly so, but you have proven yourself a worthy and interesting case. Being able to pay is also a plus as is our desire to maintain our integrity in the world market." Continuing, he said, "I also miss the days in uniform when men were soldiers and not led by politicians and corporations."

"Your airplane tickets were purchased two weeks ago for next week. You'll fly out of Athens and be met in Miami by our men."

"Thank you sir," said Conrad, "will we meet again?"

"Life is uncertain, my friend," replied the Colonel, "but it is quite possible."

Three days later, while watching television, Conrad's attention turned to the news flashing across the screen. A bank had been robbed in Rome with several injured and one casualty, the robber had escaped with an undetermined amount of cash. The police had no leads but named the casualty as an American tourist named Roger Williams.

As Conrad made preparations to leave, he wondered at the

wisdom of taking his weapons in his checked luggage. While he desired to keep them, he could also see the potential to come under scrutiny upon landing and deferred to do so. He boarded the plane at 06:00, landing in London three hours later, where he re-boarded another which was scheduled to land in Miami many hours later. The flight was without incident, making it easy for him to sleep a great deal of the way. Upon landing in Florida, he was immediately oppressed by the extremes of humidity and temperature, feeling perspiration running freely down his spine. He had little trouble at Customs and baggage inspection, showing the proper documents at the proper times and speaking only when spoken to.

The video feeds of each face were quickly analyzed by the security cameras, those of interest were directed to human personnel for further evaluation. His photo was routed electronically but then manually disregarded when upon further checking the Williams persona's information was found to have been updated to show 'deceased'. Roger Williams was no longer a person of interest.

After having retrieved his checked luggage, he had hardly moved before strong hands took the handle from him saying, "here, let me help you with that Mr. Schroeder."

Brandt's man led him to a waiting limo with a driver behind the wheel, and then joined him in the rear seat. "Welcome home, how was your flight," came the cheery question.

"Long, but relaxing," answered Conrad Schroeder.

"Are you hungry?" was the response. "It's nearly two hours to our destination."

Obviously he was to be receiving VIP treatment but the duo who had welcomed him had no idea of who he really was.

"I could eat, no hurry however, you pick the spot," Conrad said in reply. "Very well," said the man, who then leaned forward and said something in Spanish to the driver.

After having left the expressway onto a secondary highway, they headed north and west and finally turned in toward a large restaurant sitting back from the main road, with a sprinkling of vehicles in the parking lot. The driver pulled in between two unoccupied vehicles, purposely facing the limo back toward the Highway they had just left and then turned off the engine.

Neither man made any attempt to exit the vehicle until they took care to scrutinize traffic as it passed by. Obvious to Schroeder was their intent to make sure they had not been followed. They remained this way for perhaps 20 minutes before his door was opened for him and his companion in the rear seat led him toward the building. The driver stayed with the vehicle. Inside, the restaurant was impressive and well appointed, belying its outward appearance. The menu seemed to reflect a Caribbean influence but was also diverse, with the wait person more than pleased to accommodate any special requests they might receive.

Conrad had prime rib and shrimp, with a glass of Merlot, while his companion ordered two servings of a more modest fare, one to go. They made small talk while they ate, neither asking nor giving much. After a few minutes, the second dinner was served to the table to go, at which time the man excused himself before taking it with him to the car. At the car, he presented the meal to his companion with an admonishment to "stay alert," then returned to Conrad and his own meal.

Conrad was feeling more confident by the hour that the ruse had worked, he began to feel that Brandt's plan to challenge his former employers could actually succeed. His companion would not let him pay for the meal, "it has been taken care of," he said. Back at the car the man then covertly offered him a weapon, asking if it was suitable to him. Conrad knew it was no coincidence that the weapon was a Beretta 86. Colonel Brandt was still with him.

The final leg of the trip was uneventful, with the driver leaving the pavement, then taking a graveled road into the lush overgrowth, before finally coming to a stop in a clearing surrounded by tropical vegetation. The area looked much like the training camp he had recently left, with a landing pad next to one of the larger buildings. There was no visible fence but an armed guard made himself evident as they disembarked the vehicle. All three men entered the closest building, to find several more waiting for them as they entered. The presence of Mr. Smith and Mr. Jones gladdened Conrad's heart even before casting his gaze upon their leader, Colonel Brandt.

In the hours following, the Colonel brought him up to date on the events happening here at home. The journalist and his cohort had brain-stormed over many beers, linking prints from two shell casings from the murder of his friends to an international fugitive named Roger Williams. They languished to find a commonality between the well-to-do but hardly rich retirees and the wealthy Mr. Dane Adams. Once the detective began following leads, he became dogged in his investigation but did not share information with other law enforcement.

His journalist friend suggested that this was no coincidence. As they struggled to find a common denominator, they finally noted that both shared the same political visions. Thanking God for computers, they entered information concerning recent deaths of other notables in the political arena, quickly finding three which had not been investigated as homicide.

Upon further investigation and viewing the events through new eyes, the General's vehicle had shown evidence of being sideswiped.

With paint evidence sent to be analyzed and trauma to the General's person inconsistent with running into the canal, it was reopened as a homicide. Trace evidence on a hit and run case was matched to the paint on the General's vehicle. Once again, both victims were shown to have been conservatives who were politically active, financially supportive, and recently retired. With glee they knew that they had found the common thread which, when pulled, would unravel the mysteries.

The last name, E.J. Casey, who was also a wealthy political donor, had also appeared as a natural death. Mr. Casey had succumbed to heart failure while having a massage, with witnesses present. There had been no reason to assume otherwise, therefore no criminal investigation had followed. The only evidence at the scene had been his personal possessions and a water bottle. Blood tests had shown no drugs or alcohol in his system. However, with insight and motive apparent, the detective re-interviewed the staff at the spa, finding Mr. Cameron Smith, a dear "friend" of Mr. Casey, had been present just prior to his arrival, but had left suddenly feeling ill, never to return. The investigation then focused on the water bottle, which showed evidence of a toxic cocktail capable of causing heart failure and the now familiar finger prints of the mysterious Roger Williams.

Both the journalist and the detective knew this was big. They also knew that they were in this way over their heads. Making duplicates of the entire investigation, with instruction to have a copy delivered to the state's attorney general in case of their death, the detective reached out to an old friend in the FBI. Without revealing the reason for asking, he inquired if his friend had ever come across the name of Roger Williams in his job.

The man's ears pricked up noticeably at the mention of the name, then he said, "yes, he was the hot potato in the department for several months. Everyone was looking for him and no one knew why. Why do you ask?"

The detective played it down saying, "name came up in a murder investigation, but went nowhere."

"Not surprised," commented the agent. "He was killed in a bank heist in Rome recently, case closed."

The detective now turned his attention away from Williams, focusing instead on why the crimes were committed and who benefitted. He began actively listening to the political commentators in the media while his protégé interviewed them regarding their opinions of how the political climate had changed with Dane's death. He gleaned a great deal of information in short order, his spotlight coming to focus on several key liberals in leadership.

He also learned that there was a quiet investigation going on within the intelligence community which paralleled his own. He now remembered when once, a couple of men in dark suits with dark glasses, had warned him off, saying that he was outside of his authority and to stop asking questions. That, of course, made him all the more eager to 'out' the bad guys.

Conrad, with his support troops, drove northward together, the Colonel being frequently updated from his sources as additional information came in. Both the FBI and CIA had started internal investigations to determine why they had been involved in the "Williams" affair and from whom had come the orders. As Brandt had anticipated, there was no honor among thieves, with cover-ups and finger pointing already in full swing.

About this time the journalist 'leaked' the first part of his story, showing that a conspiracy had been discovered linking the several deaths together. As Washington went crazy trying to cover its soiled linen, the defensive line broke down with some minor participants offering information in return for amnesty.

William Barker had left the White House for the day, and had returned home alone to his prestigious mansion in Virginia. He could feel his world falling apart but held out hope of finding a scapegoat to take the heat, as he had done in the past. For the right consideration, an underling may take full credit for the operation, spending a short time in prison, then being pardoned by a new and grateful President after the dust had settled. As he entered the house he became aware of a presence inside, having no wife, and with the domestics off for the evening, he was greatly alarmed. He reached into his jacket and pulled out his Glock 21 and chambered a round as he moved deeper into the house.

"Bill," came the voice. "It's probably not a good idea to pull a weapon. You are poorly trained to use it. That is why you hire others to do your wet work."

Barker's heart went cold as he immediately recognized the Colonel's voice. He dropped his arm, still holding the gun, to his side, then looked around, making eye contact with Brandt. Stepping through the door behind him were Smith, Jones, and Roger Williams/Schmidt. Barker's jaw went slack as a smile spread across their faces.

They were not unknown to him, he had used them previously in their country's service, and then when it became expedient to do so, had sold them out, used them as scapegoats. Disgraced and humiliated, they had been forced to leave their country for other, less honorable service.

"Well, Bill," the Colonel resumed. "Where do you go from here?" "Federal prison and maybe finally finding yourself a lover? I've always questioned why you weren't married."

Barker glowered without answering, then said, "Is there a way out of this?"

Brandt smiled as he answered. "You're holding it, Bill. Question is, do you have the balls to use it?"

Alternate ending 1:

Barker lifted his arm as he turned toward them, bringing his sight to bear on Schroeder. As he squeezed the trigger, three additional reports simultaneously shook the room. Schroeder first sagged, then fell to the floor, his blood pooling around his lifeless body. Across the room, Barker also fell, three holes venting his life's blood into his expensive carpet. Brandt, Smith, and Jones turned without a word and left without looking back.

Alternate ending 2:

Barker, with a resigned, yet melancholy half smile, raised the Glock, slowly placing it under his chin. Without further conversation he gently pulled the trigger, ending his reign of self-serving abuse of authority. His four adversaries watched him crumple soundlessly to the carpet before leaving without comment or conversation.

Alternate ending 3:

The men left, leaving Barker standing alone in his foyer, gun hanging limply in his hand, disgrace and remorse written across his face. Their work was done here. The wolves were hungry for Barker's blood. They were closing in on him and would take down their prey while toppling the country's leadership in the process. Gerhardt was now willing to give himself up, to ask God for forgiveness, and to let justice determine his earthly destiny.

The End

The Trigger

Prologue

Don't think that the unspeakable has not already been spoken of, considered and reconsidered by your leaders, and that plans may well be under way to implement it ~ dan

~   ~

Some wondered at the statistics while others questioned their accuracy, but few considered it any more than an anomaly that the increase in the numbers of cancer deaths among the elderly would triple in such a short time. Researchers worked to find a common denominator... occupation, diet, lifestyle, environmental factors, or anything that would tie them together to explain the monumental rise in deaths among America's senior population. It was not a single form of cancer that was striking the population, but across the board, all forms had seen a vast increase in a short time span.

Ichiro was an American-born Japanese with a keen analytical mind and a passion for unlocking the secrets of which only God holds the keys. At the tender age of 24, he held a doctorate in micro-biology and was a rising star in his field. It was widely considered by those on the inside that the unlocking of the human genome had paved the way for research that held the answers to the cause of the abnormal growth in human cells loosely termed "cancer." Most also believed that the answer had already been found but constrained by the money-hungry cancer treatment centers and pharmaceutical industry and others that profited from human illness.

The term 'trigger' was the one used to describe the proximate cause of all cancers, the event that provided the signal to the cells to replicate abnormally. It was for this trigger that millions of dollars and man-hours had been spent over many decades, and it was this that Ichiro believed he'd found.

He was uneasy, wary, even guarded in his optimism as he checked and rechecked his results, but in the end Ichiro was forced to accept that for which he had hoped for, even prayed for, was true.

He had discovered the 'trigger' for cancer and was well on his way to finding a way to use it to prevent cancer from happening. What he had discovered was that nearly 100% of humans contained the trigger, just waiting to be pulled.

~ ~

"How close is he?" Anson asked into the encrypted telephone.

"Very close," came the almost whispered reply. "He's meticulous, he probably has had it for some time but is diligent in rechecking his work before announcing it."

"What will happen when he does?" Anson asked, though already knowing the answer.

"First, disbelief, then excitement as the scientific community pours over it to verify his findings, and finally a Nobel Prize and our world will forever change," the hushed voice said.

"That cannot happen," Anson insisted. "The world has too much riding on the status quo, and now our own government has become a player as well."

"I am awaiting your instructions," the voice replied dispassionately. "Although I am sure you know that Pandora's Box has been opened and if not he, someone else will come forward with the cure."

"Give me time to discuss the matter with the Director and I'll get back to you," Anson said, breaking the connection.

~   ~

The pushing of vaccinations upon the senior segment of society gradually became mainstream and well accepted. It became the question of the day in retirement centers, nursing homes, and care centers across the nation... "Have you gotten your flu shot, your pneumonia shot, or your shingles shot yet?"

It had been easy to build a near hysteria into their ranks by using the liberal media to spread the news of deaths of the seniors from preventable causes. Everyone, regardless of age, wanted to believe they could live forever. Working hand-in-hand with Congress, the current administration had gained popularity with their programs to subsidize the cost of the inoculations, at taxpayer expense. Who doesn't enjoy a freebie when some unknown is picking up the tab?

It seemed to Anson that hardly anyone worked within the framework of the established government agencies anymore. First, the CIA had found it necessary for the greater good, to create the black bag ops department that technically had no political oversight. The FBI had necessarily followed suit, but with far less fanfare, and finally the Homeland security, who seemed to answer to no one but the President, operated in a manner inconsistent with the Constitution of the Republic which it served. Anson was amazed and pleased at how far they had come so quickly. The nation, for which he had pledged his allegiance, was to him a fat lazy sleeping dog that cared not who put the food in its dish as long as it was there.

Anson represented a non-existent liberal charity who received its funding from large medical providers including hospitals, treatment facilities, pharmaceutical manufacturers, hospice and even some mortuaries, in exchange for tax considerations. The oversight was solely at the discretion of the IRS who was under the control of the current administration, that looked at Medicare and social security benefits as a burden that crippled its other expansive entitlement programs.

Nothing, either written or verbal, came down the chain of command from the White House, nothing that could be documented later to embarrass the ruling party. The mission, however, had been carefully mapped out for Anson right there in the Oval office under the very noses of Congress. There was no ambiguity about the message that was clearly delivered. The "specially manufactured" vaccines were distributed to the retired and soon to be retired, ages 60 and over. Then nothing more needed to be done but to let nature take its course.

Recent federal legislation had limited Medicare's financial participation at age 70 when the results of the cancer would be at their most critical stages. Many, however, died while receiving treatment under their own insurance providers and before they were able to utilize Medicare or draw their first social security check.

The program had now been in full swing for nearly two years, with the government financing ads for the elderly to take advantage of its subsidies and receive the vaccines to prevent the three dreaded diseases. Meanwhile, the supportive industries stuffed their coffers while more and more seniors continued to be diagnosed and die.

~   ~

Ichiro stopped and removed his shoes at the door, both out of habit and as a gesture of respect for his parents, who still clung to their heritage. As he entered their comfortable home, he took pleasure in its familiarity. His diminutive mother and father, neither over five feet, were seated together on their sofa with a soft music playing in the background as he greeted them with a word and a bow. They greeted him in turn, but he noted that neither looked well or happy.

With an IQ near genius, Ichiro was still remarkably average in many ways, unlike some who had little in the way of common sense, he did not live in 'Netherland' nor did he march to a 'different drummer' as did many men of his stature. He was quick to recognize real life situations and common, everyday problems and to attend to them as necessary.

The few friends he did have were not those from the laboratory but ones from high school and the neighborhood here where he had grown up. Had it been otherwise he'd not have noticed the dark sedan parked awkwardly at the curb down the block in front of the Jones' house, while the other neighbors always parked in their driveways. He took note, memorized the license plate number and went about his business.

Haru, Ichiro's father, had been an optometrist for nearly forty years before finally bowing to age and taking retirement the previous fall at age 70. Akiko, his mother, had always been the dutiful wife and mother in a most traditional way.

"Father," Ichiro asked, "are you and mother not well?"

"Very tired, my son," he answered. "Maybe we have gotten a touch of the flu."

"How long have you not felt well?" he asked.

His father shrugged, then answered, "a few days, maybe a week."

It was only now that he could see the obvious decline in the look of vigor and vitality which they had always seemed to enjoy.

"Please allow me to check those things for which I have been trained," Ichiro said. He removed his medical bag from a nearby closet and moved toward them.

So small, and suddenly so old and fragile, he thought to himself as though seeing them for the first time. He carefully removed the stethoscope that he'd owned since college and listened to the steady but elevated beat of his father's heart. Having the equivalent of a medical degree but without the credentials that went with a medical practice, he struggled to remember some of the more mundane features of a physical exam.

As he listened down his father's back, the sounds of crackling cellophane became apparent as the old man breathed in and out. Pneumonia was his instant diagnosis. It was obvious to him that his father had a respiratory illness. The BP cuff indicated a slightly elevated reading but within acceptable ranges.

Ichiro repeated the procedure on his mother, who seemed to tremble at his gentle touch. He spoke reassuringly to her in her native tongue as he explained each of his necessary encroachments into her personal space. He heard no sounds of respiratory illness but noticed a marked color change in her lips and gums and possible swelling of the tongue. Of course, without tests, he was far out of his element as a medical provider but became insistent that they submit themselves to more advanced tests. He assured them that the costs would be born by their Medicare provider, leaving them little out of pocket expense.

~ ~

"Bob, this is Ichiro," the young scientist said into the phone, "I need a favor."

"Of course," Ichiro's superior said pleasantly. "What may I do for you?"

Bob, Robert Beckwith to those outside of the inner circle, was the research department head, who now nearing retirement, tried hard to remember when he was one of the "young guns" eager to unlock the secrets of the universe.

"I need the name of a competent and compassionate physician who will see my parents right away without any of the normal referral hierarchy," Ichiro said. "I believe my father has advanced respiratory infection and mother seems suddenly quite anemic."

"Who is their regular physician?" the older man asked matter-of-factly.

"They do not have one, they have until late always used traditional Japanese methods." Ichy replied. "I've never known either to have as much as a head cold until now."

Bob hesitated a moment while he thought, then answered. "Let me make a few calls and get right back to you."

"Thank you," the younger man said.

Later the same afternoon the phone in the lab rang, it was Bob.

"Dr. Masako Fujiyama," Bob said. "He worked with me when I first started in research. He went into private practice a dozen years ago and has agreed as a favor to see your parents this week. I'll get his contact information over to you right away."

Ichiro let out his breath, and then said, "Bob, you'll never know how much I appreciate this."

Bob laughed softly, "You owe me lunch, Boy Genius. My wife and I are praying for you," he added before hanging up the receiver.

Ichiro made little progress in his work, having spent a good part of the day on the phone arranging an appointment with the doctor's office and the rest reassuring his parents that they should keep it.

~   ~

"Anson," he said into the encrypted phone that he kept with him at all times.

"We've had him under surveillance for a week now with nothing new to report," the voice replied. "Just last night we finished bugging his lab."

"Stay on it, I want to know every time he goes to the head," Anson replied curtly before hanging up.

~ ~

Ichiro took the first personal day off in the three years he'd worked at the lab to drive his parents to meet their new doctor. It had taken all of his persuasive power just to get them into the car and almost a threat to get them out and into the office. They were greeted by a young attractive oriental in her mid-twenties who then reverted to Japanese as she welcomed them and asked them to fill out the HIPAA forms and have a seat. Both handed their clip boards to their son without conversation. Point made, Ichiro thought, they're only here to please me and nothing more.

"Mr. and Mrs. Ito," an efficient blond thirty-something with a big smile said, "would you please follow me?"

Both stood before Haru spoke, "We'd like to have our son join us also."

"Of course," she answered cordially, "please come this way."

The three followed the nurse into the doctor's expansive office where she showed them to a seat and handed several forms to the doctor seated behind the desk. He stood, gave them a traditional bow, and then said in Japanese, "I am honored to meet you."

Both Haru and Akiko smiled back and replied in kind.

"Ichiro, your work I hear should make your parents proud," he added, addressing the younger man directly. "Bob speaks very highly of you."

Both of Ichy's parents beamed at the compliment.

The verbal interview went on for nearly an hour, the doctor asking each very pointed questions and making notes. No mention was made of moving to an examination room which Ichiro supposed was the doctor's way of making the environment less threatening to his parents.

Doctor Masako addressed Haru with respect, "From your own years in practice you already know that certain tests must be made to evaluate your condition and to make proper recommendations."

Haru nodded and smiled at his wife. "It is so," he affirmed to her.

The doctor stood, removed a stethoscope from his desk and moved around the desk. He made no attempt to approach until invited to do so. He repeated the process that Ichiro had done, making additional notes as he did so, smiling at each of them and speaking soothingly in Japanese.

"With your permission," he said, "I'll ask my nurse to take a blood sample from each of you."

Both nodded their heads, but neither moved. The nurse returned in response to the doctor's buzzer and asked the couple to join her in an exam room. Ichiro remained in his seat across from the doctor until the door closed, then leaned forward and said, "thank you, Doctor, for your kindness and tact, and I fear they may possibly have something serious going on that they are not aware of."

The doctor nodded agreement and replied, "yes, there seems to be a marked change in their overall health in a short period of time. It is wise that we determine its cause." Then he added, "Bob did not share the nature of your work with me, what is your area of expertise?

Ichiro was embarrassed that the more experienced man would consider that he'd have an area of expertise at his young age, but smiled wanly and answered, "I am pursuing the cause of cancer."

Inscrutable, as the Caucasians would term it, the Japanese doctor seemed to show no emotion or surprise but took the offered information in stride. "And how," he asked, "is your work coming?"

At this point Ichiro abandoned his humble stature, smiled broadly and answered with enthusiasm, "I think I may have found it! No one knows yet since I have been carefully rechecking my results, but it appears that I may have really found it."

Remembering his own time in research and the enthusiasm he held during his youth, the doctor was careful to not encourage or discourage the young man sitting across from him. "What kind of cancer?" he asked quietly.

"All cancer," Ichiro answered. "I believe cancer in its many forms is begun by a common trigger which causes cells to divide irrationally."

The doctor showed interest openly, then asked, "And where did you find the keys to the castle?"

"Right in plain sight where God put it," Ichiro answered, "the human genome, I believe holds the answers to nearly all of man's illnesses." He went on to describe in technical terms the many rabbit trails that he had pursued before finding the one that would possibly yield the answers to mankind's most deadly enemy.

Dr. Fujiyama immediately showed interest and excitement in his young colleague's discovery, then suggested, "perhaps we could have lunch together and discuss this in more detail."

Ichiro nodded, then said, "please do keep our conversations private until I am able to confirm the results and share them with my employers."

Masako returned the nod of compliance.

A gentle knock on the door was heard before it was opened to re-admit Haru and Akiko by the nurse. Ichiro rose to join them as the doctor stood and dismissed them graciously, promising to convey the results to them as soon as they were available. On the return trip home, they visited the pharmacy where they picked up the prescribed antibiotic for Haru's suspected pneumonia.

~   ~

The following day Ichiro was working in the lab when he took a call from Fujiyama's office.

"Can you meet me today for lunch?" the doctor asked with urgency in his voice, "I have something for you."

"Yes, of course," Ichiro answered, a sense of dread settling on him like a weight. They agreed to meet at a bistro nearby and then disconnected.

Masako was waiting at an outside table when Ichiro arrived, a small insulated cooler sat on the chair beside him. He neither rose nor smiled but gestured to a seat. Trepidation elevated Ichiro's heart beat and blood pressure as his mind presented one possible scenario after another. He sat and took the older man's hand.

"The news is not good," the doctor said plainly, "I have brought you blood samples for your own inspection and the results of our own diagnosis. Your father seems to have an aggressive form of lung cancer and your mother's blood count shows a marked decrease in red blood cells and a high white count, pointing to the possibility of leukemia."

Ichiro's heart sank, possibly because he knew far better than most what the future held for most with the same diagnosis. He could see sadness in the older man's eyes when he was handed the refrigerated blood samples. They shook hands and walked away without further conversation.

He walked the several blocks back to the lab with the weight of his burden threatening to crush him. "Oh Jesus," he cried out silently, "please let this not be so."

There is a marked difference between a vaccine for and a cure for a disease; the one prevents a disease from happening, the other addresses it after it has opportunity to attack and injure the victim. Ichiro was on the threshold, possibly of prevention, but maybe still months or years from finding a cure.

~ ~

"Bob, I need to see you right away," Ichiro said into the telephone's answering machine. He'd called knowing that his boss was probably already at lunch or in a meeting with the brass.

He'd hardly ended the call when his cell rang back, it was Bob. "Come right over, I've just finished a sandwich at my desk and had put the phone on record."

By the time Ichiro had left his friend's office he had unburdened himself with the announcement of his possible discovery as well as the results of his parent's medical diagnosis. He'd asked and had been granted to work exclusively on the project, hoping to take his discovery forward to its ultimate goal of finding a cure. Unknown to both, Anson had ears in the office which promptly reported the new development directly to him.

"It is God's will," Haru said, without emotion or fear. "He is in control of all things." Akiko nodded, after hearing the news their son brought home with him, but with less conviction than her husband. Both of them had found peace and salvation in Jesus many years before and had brought Ichiro up in faith as well. All were pleased to share their personal testimonies with any who would listen.

Ichiro found himself working eighteen-hour days, catching sleep when possible, and providing transportation and support as his parents entered the traditional treatment world of cancer medicine. Akiko was being transfused three times a week with red blood cells harvested from aphaeresis donors, and Haru's body was fighting the effects of pneumonia brought on by the mutant cells in the lung tissue.

On a positive note, the results of Ichido's work were confirmed by a separate team led by Bob himself, but not yet announced to the world.

The incidence of cancer among seniors continued to rise without medical explanation while the CDC and other agencies searched feverishly for a cause without success.

"Anson," he said into the phone, while listening attentively to the voice on the other end, "what do you have to report?"

~ ~

"Cat's out of the bag," came the answer. "He told his superior and they have confirmed what we had suspected, he has discovered the trigger."

"Will it lead to a cure?" Anson asked pointedly.

"Our people have yet to find one and they have had a two year head start," the voice answered, "but our boy is motivated and intelligent, who can tell?"

"Who do we have on the inside?" Anson asked.

"Bell," was the one word answer. "Retired CIA with a biomedical degree, well known and accepted in the lab."

"Good," answered Anson. "Let him know I expect him to keep us informed, meanwhile I'll speak with those upstairs and see what they want to do." He ended the call without pleasantries.

Anson wasted no time in contacting his superiors in Washington who wasted no time in contacting the participating pharmaceutical companies producing the 'spiked' vaccines.

"Are you on top of this?" came the question from the President's

Chief of Staff, "or should we be looking to someone else to handle this problem?"

Anson's ego nearly caused him to push back before he realized that tact was the path which would gain him the most ground.

"Have I never not been able to handle my end?" he asked in return. "We are on top of it and will do whatever is necessary to achieve our common goals."

"See that you do," was the reply before disconnection.

Anson was troubled, not by the indiscriminate spreading of slow death by the government that had sworn to serve their constituents, but by the spiraling dimension of the project that touched nearly every life in some fashion. Those on the medical side who were not complicit were making millions while truly believing they were treating the victim's interests to the best of their abilities. Even those big companies who were not insiders made fortunes while doing increased business.

Citizens on the street who invested in the industry doubled and tripled their dollars when Congress passed tax legislation to treat such income more favorably to stimulate the economy. The party in power gained seats in off-year elections as a result and looked for another term in the country's highest office. Everyone seemed to benefit except those families whose elderly were dying in droves. There seemed no end to it, nothing or no one big enough to stop it.

~   ~

As it often is with mankind, the road that lies ahead is not seen to its conclusion, leaving us guessing where it goes and what stops it provides along the way. Ichiro, having found the key to the cause of abnormal cell growth, worked feverishly to determine how to stop it from happening. Ichy wondered if there was but one trigger, could there also be a single cause or finger that pulled the trigger, what mechanism God had built in to the once immortal body to limit its life span.

All over the Old Testament were reports of men living hundreds of years without the aid of medical science, but then the time came when God had determined that the median age would be about 70, Ichiro questioned what had changed. It was much like chasing the mist to determine the purposes of the Almighty God and he knew it. All he could do was to trust and use that which God had given him to try and find an answer.

His mother's condition worsened while it seemed that his father's had slightly improved using conventional medicine. Ichiro prayed faithfully that God might shackle the beast that threatened their lives while he worked to find a solution. Remission was a word used often when God has determined that we need a temporary rest from our struggles. He prayed for remission.

Bob entered the lab and motioned Ichiro into a vacant office.

"Ichiro," he said, "I think the time has come to announce your discovery and open it up to the scientific world so they can aid you in your race to find a cure."

The young scientist was torn, knowing that his boss was right in one respect, and knowing that his life's work would become the property of others. He immediately caught himself, pride had entered the equation, and he wanted to be the one who found it, but why, so he could take credit? He asked God to forgive him.

"You are right of course," he answered. "Sometimes we forget our goal and focus on ourselves. The sooner others join us in the search the sooner we find a cure."

~ ~

When Anson heard the conversation played back, he knew the time had come to take action.

"Tell Bell," he said into the phone, "I want the lab burned to the ground, nothing left standing, and no leads as to how it happened. If possible I'd like to have those two inside when it goes down."

"Done," was the one word response.

~ ~

"It has to look like an accident," the voice emphasized as Bell listened. "No trace of foul play, nothing to lead investigators anywhere."

"Noted," Bell replied. "Give me a day or so to work out the details."

"You don't have a day or two," the voice on the phone said harshly, "they are going to break the news any time now."

Bell was a talented researcher in his own right, but his interest was not to provide for the universal good of mankind, but rather packing away a tidy sum in an off-shore account for the day when he hoped to step away from his employers.

He was kidding himself, he knew, because few ever just leave such a job and live happily ever after. He'd left the CIA in disgrace after they had ousted him for trafficking munitions for his own profit. He'd looked at it as moonlighting, they had seen it in a completely different light.

"Meet me in the lab at 7:00," the text message on Bob's phone read, "I've made a break-through, signed Ichiro."

Another, only slightly different, that was left on Ichiro's phone when he failed to pickup, was signed Bob.

Bell damaged the feed lines to the bunsen burners in the main lab, disabled the gas monitoring devices, and set the quirk device on the thermostat to provide the spark when the temperature reached 72°, then disabled the unlocking device on both exit doors. He parked in the main parking lot several hundred yards away but with a clear view of the complex and waited as the clock ticked. At twenty minutes until seven he watched as Bob's Peugeot stopped at the security gate before being waved through. There was no sign of Ichiro's Camry when the second story windows blew outward and a ball of fire followed. He could only hope that his young colleague had parked in the rear and made the rendezvous on time. He was, however, certain that every shred of evidence and all data concerning the project had been destroyed.

Ichiro was eating breakfast when he opened the morning paper and read, "Gas leak in research lab kills two and injures a score of others." He automatically reached for his phone to call Bob but found he had left it in his car the previous night. The oversight was far out of character for the young man who depended on the device for every-thing.

When he arrived at the complex there were still fire engines and police cars everywhere. Rescue crews were sifting through the wreck-age, looking for possible survivors and victims. Distraught faces, both known and unknown to him, stood about in silence, some with tears on their cheeks. A tall, dark haired man with a notebook was walking among them asking questions and taking notes. Ichiro tried again to reach Bob on his cell but got no answer. It was then that he noticed the message left the previous evening. Almost like a voice from beyond Bob's message drew him to it. Bob had attempted to bring him here and had been killed in the blast.

"Ichiro," a voice said. "Thank God you are alright. Have you heard what happened?"

Ichy looked up dispassionately into the eyes of his co-worker, Max Bell. For a moment he could not speak, could not think, and could not grasp what he was feeling.

"They say Bob and the night guard were killed instantly and several others are seriously injured," Bell volunteered. "Heard something about a gas leak."

Still Ichiro didn't speak, his mind running full out trying to grasp what he was seeing. His best friend gone, his works destroyed, and close friends taken away to the burn center. Then he settled on a single sentence, "something about a gas leak." His mind objected, a gas leak couldn't happen, double and triple automatic safety shutoffs were installed to prevent just this sort of happening. If it was gas, it must be an intentional act. Terrorists, certainly not, there was nothing here that resembled weaponry or research into that field. In the background he could still hear Max chattering away but ignored his efforts to make conversation.

As he turned to walk back to his car, a firm hand grasped his arm. "Do you work here?" the dark haired man asked.

"I do... I did," Ichiro corrected himself. "The second floor was where my lab used to be."

The man looked at the badge which hung loosely around Ichiro's neck. "Ichiro Ito," he said, writing the name down on the pad. "What is it you do here?"

"I'm in bio-medical research," he replied. "I'm a project leader. Who are you?" he added, after regaining his composure.

"Special Agent Mike Stout, FBI," the larger man said, flashing his credentials. "Tell me Mr. Project leader, what were you working on?"

Ichiro hesitated but then found keeping his secret ludicrous so he answered honestly, "we were working on a cure for cancer."

Ichiro could see the man almost laugh at the idea that this young Japanese lab rat would presume to tackle such a monumental task.

"You and a hundred thousand other people," he scoffed. Who was that you were talking to before I walked up, one of your crew?"

"No, his name is Max Bell, he works in a different department,"

Ichiro clarified, "I hardly know him."

"Looks to me like Bell got out without any injuries," the agent replied.

"He wasn't in the building," Ichiro said, "he works the day shift. He would have been off last night."

The agent gave him a strange look but said nothing further.

"He told me he heard that they suspect a gas leak," Ichy said. "That cannot be true. There are too many monitors and failsafes for that to happen accidently."

The agent drew him aside and asked, "what are you saying? Why would someone blow up a medical research facility?"

Ichy shrugged, "I do not know," he answered. "What I do know is that this was a perfect storm and few things are perfect."

Before they could continue their conversation another agent approached and began talking quietly with agent Stout. Ichiro turned and began walking toward his car but was hailed by the agent. "May I have your phone number Mr. Ito, I'd like to continue our conversation at a later time."

Ichiro walked back and handed the agent his business card, then continued to his car. Bell was leaning against his car when he arrived.

"Who was that you were talking to?" he asked. "Some fire inspector?"

"No," Ichy answered, sounding annoyed by Bell's questions. "Some FBI guy named Stout."

"Oh yeah? What'd you tell him?" Bell pressed. "Did you tell him about the call?"

"I just told him I thought it was impossible that it would happen by accident," Ichy replied while getting into his car. "It's hard for me to believe it really happened, years of work gone and my best friend too."

Ichy put the Toyota into gear and pulled away leaving Bell standing in the lot alone.

~ ~

"Knucklehead," Anson stormed into the phone at Bell. "Can't you be trusted with one small thing? It's no wonder you washed out with the company, you can't even take out one Jap!"

Bell responded, "maybe it is for the best, all of his work is gone, he can't hurt us, and maybe I can hang the explosion on him."

"Take care of him, one way or the other I don't want to hear from him again," Anson said with conviction before hanging up.

~ ~

That night the fire was all over the news. They reported that the only thing that saved the entire structure was the sprinkler system. Ichiro lay awake picturing the explosion, his friend in a ball of flames with no chance of survival, waiting for him to arrive. Why had he gone there and thought what was so important that he'd summoned Ichiro to join him, just before sleep took him in its arms.

The clock read 2:17 a.m. when Ichiro woke with a start. He was wide awake, Bell's words filling his mind, *did you tell him about the call?* Ichiro went carefully back over their conversations remembering nothing about mentioning Bob's call to him. How had he known if he'd not sent the message himself, and to what purpose? He lay awake until dawn, then showered quietly without waking his parents and went to the phone book.

In the government pages under FBI he found several numbers, none local. He called the 800 number and asked for Special Agent Mike Stout. As expected, the reply came that Agent Stout was not available, but could they take a number and have him return the call. Ichy gave them his cell and filled a bowl with cereal and poured himself a glass of cold milk while he waited.

About a quarter of ten the phone rang, it was Stout. Ichiro reminded him of their earlier visit and suggested they meet to discuss some things that had just come to light regarding the explosion. When Stout tried to pursue the discussion over the phone, Ichy refused, saying he preferred to meet in person.

At twelve fifteen, Ichiro was sitting at the same table he and Bob has occupied the previous week when Stout walked up and took a seat beside him.

"You watch too many spy movies," Stout said smiling, "this is not how we do it in the real world."

"How do you do it then?" Ichiro asked returning the smile. "We are being watched, and yes I am sure of it."

Without thinking Stout swiveled his head around looking for surveillance but saw none.

"Nice job, Agent Stout," Ichy said reprovingly. "Now they know that we know they are watching."

Stout looked down sheepishly and did not argue the point. "What is so important that we could not discuss it on the phone?" he asked a little too loudly.

Ichiro told the agent of the mysterious phone message from Bob and of Bell's inquiry about their conversation before ending with his suspicions that he had been watched for several weeks prior to the explosion. Covertly he put his cell on the table turning it so that Bob's message was displayed.

This time the agent seemed to take him seriously and suggested that he may still be in danger and may have been the target of the bombing for some yet-to-be-discovered reason. Ichiro nodded but said only, "So Agent Stout, where do we begin?"

"We begin by providing you some protection while we try and sort out to whom you pose a threat," Stout said. "And... please call me Mike."

Across the courtyard in a non-descript sedan with out-of-state plates, two men took photos of the occupants of the bistro and aimed their parabolic microphone at two men who were deep in conversation.

~   ~

By God's province Ichiro had taken home his laptop and several flash drives with him when he left the lab, intending to work a few hours from home. They remained locked in his trunk and forgotten until a week after the explosion when he ran an errand to the market for his mother. His first inclination was to remove them and begin his work anew, his second was to contact Mike and have them copied in their entirety and placed in safe keeping.

Haru seemed to be making progress in his battle with his illness while Akiko was on the wane in spite of transfusions and monumental efforts to push her cancer into remission. Three weeks had gone by and just now the repairs to the lab were beginning, following an in-depth investigation by the FBI and local authorities. Ichiro felt helpless and useless sitting idly by, with little to do.

"Ichy," Mike said jovially over the phone, "let's have lunch, I have something to tell you."

"Where?" Ichiro responded.

"You'll need to come my way this time, to the Federal Building, I'll order in," the agent said.

When he arrived Mike was waiting with a visitor's pass with his name and photo on it. He didn't ask where they had gotten the photo.

Mike put his finger to his lips and led them to the third floor and into an unoccupied room. "The room is secure," Mike finally said. "It has been swept twice."

Ichiro thought at first he was being put on for his remarks about the surveillance at the bistro, then realized Mike was serious.

"We've got some big players in this thing," Mike confided. "Big money with high connections. People who can stonewall even the FBI. Please tell me all you can about your research, don't leave out a thing."

Ichiro spoke with Mike and to the VOR recorder for over an hour before he paused to take a drink. Mike was taking copious notes and asking questions as he went. Finally he turned off the recorder and handed Ichy a hero sandwich and chips and said, "your buddy Bell is ex-CIA, we think he's turned hired gun, most likely he was the one sent to take you out."

Ichy nearly choked on his sandwich. "But why?" he asked. "It makes no sense. Who would care if I discovered a cure?"

A light went on in Mike's head, bells rang, and a smile graced his countenance. "Who indeed," he said. "Only everyone in the world that profits from illness and death from cancer."

~　~

Bell's body was found by two grouse hunters a hundred yards off the main highway a week later with two holes in the back of his head.

~　~

Akiko was taken by ambulance to the ER and admitted to ICU where chemo seemed to hurt more than it helped her aged body. Haru slept at her side, leaving only to shower and change clothes. Ichiro was alone at their house but felt the presence of his unseen protectors both day and night. He visited the hospital daily, then worked into the night on his laptop, retracing the steps that he had taken more than a month before. Finally he was able to recreate the entire double-helix model in its entirety, including the elusive trigger, the mitochondrial genome he had numbered ZX215.

Having accomplished a great deal, but sadly no closer to finding the "cure" than before the explosion; he turned his focus to a huge volume of information about the victims which had been provided by the CDC. That personal information of each included a wealth of information about their personal lives both before and after being diagnosed with the various forms of cancer.

As he perused case files, it became apparent that he'd never find a common denominator alone, he needed help. Ichiro spent three days working nearly day and night setting the parameters and programming his computer to search and sort through the millions of bits of information. Then he slept for 18 hours while it did its work.

Akiko took a turn for the worse as her kidneys shut down and was forced to go on dialysis. The battle for life was seemingly a futile exercise, but still she fought to stay alive. Haru, no doubt from the emotional demands on him and additional stress and worry, seemed to be failing as well.

~ ~

"Ichy," Mike said while sitting at the kitchen table in the Ito home, "we have found direct evidence that the explosion was not an accident and that your team was the target of the crime. It is logical to surmise that Bell was the conspirator and was later killed after he failed his mission to eliminate you."

Ichiro nodded having deduced as much himself and continued to enjoy his breakfast cereal.

"Sometimes you can tell as much from what you cannot access as from what you can," the agent went on. "Every time I hit a stonewall I look to who has built it and who benefits from it. When the FBI is denied access to information I look to who has the clout to make that happen."

Mike now had Ichiro's full attention.

"Okay Mike," the young man said. "That makes sense and the profit motive does as well, but how could they foresee the increase in the incident rates unless they could control them?"

He had just finished the sentence when the light blinked on, "they found the trigger... didn't they?"

Mike nodded. "Yes, it appears that they have," he agreed, "but how did it become so widespread so quickly?"

"I'm working on that," Ichy answered, "or I should say the computer is. I should have some answers very soon."

He leaned over to pick up his napkin from the floor just as his mother's tea pot exploded on the counter behind him. Mike joined him on the kitchen floor while pulling his service weapon and surveying the area. A large jagged hole in the dining room window testified of a single shot into the area where they had been sitting. The two agents who had shadowed Ichiro for over a month had heard the report of the weapon and ran to the residence from their vehicle just as Mike opened the front door.

"Anyone hurt?" the first asked Mike as they entered.

Mike shook his head. "Where'd it come from," he asked.

"Behind us, maybe somewhere over on the next block, from the sound of it," the agent said.

His partner nodded agreement. "From the angle it must have come from an elevated position," he added.

Mike smiled at his new friend, then said, "Let's keep the curtains closed from now on. Ichiro returned the smile and nodded.

Obviously Ichiro and his pursuit of the cure was still viewed as a threat by those who had blown up the lab. A barely audible beep emitted from Ichy's powerful little laptop signaling that it had completed its assigned tasks. He went to it and began to view the results while Mike stood looking over his shoulder.

Working backward from the present, the computer had begun its computations when the first noticeable increases in the incidence of cancer began, roughly 18 months before. The incidence rate had climbed exponentially since then to its current rate of 76% for those over 65 who were diagnosed with one form or another of cancer. Looking back five years, the rate had been under 20%.

Ichiro took time to point out to Mike what he was seeing and its relevance to the trigger research. He paged forward to where the statistics were compared with a multitude of factors including race, geographical location, employment, and medical histories. Race, location, and past employment seemed to have played no part in the increased stats, but when they came to medical histories a particular area clearly manifested itself, "immunizations."

There was a direct correlation of those immunized for shingles, pneumonia, and influenza. The incidence rate of diagnosed cancer among the three categories was over 80%. Mike was amazed and excited at the same time.

"You've found it!" he exclaimed excitedly. "Someone has spiked their vaccines."

Ichiro was also convinced but less emotional when he said, "and now what can we do about it?"

~ ~

"I think you got him," one of the assailants said to the shooter, "I saw him fall from his chair. Let's get out of here."

They removed the huge scope from the weapon and broke it down into a waiting rifle case before policing the area for any evidence which might tie them to the shooting. Slowly and carefully they closed the second story window and went down the stairs and out the back of the vacant house. Their sedan was parked in the alley ready to provide their escape. They pulled away and had nearly made it to the cross street when a black and white with lights flashing pulled across their pathway. The rear view showed another likewise was pulling in behind them.

Professionals yes, but sloppy and not prepared for the quick response the police and FBI had provided. They were taken into federal custody in separate cars, finger printed, and jailed separately. Both carried handguns, one of which was quickly tied to Bell's execution, again sloppy work to not have disposed of the weapon. Both were charged with conspiracy to commit murder, complicity in a terrorist act, and wrongful death of un-named plaintiffs, those being the victims of the cancer scheme.

For the first two hours neither man spoke, neither showed emotion nor fear. But when Mike posed the question to them why they thought their employers would hesitate to have them killed any more than they had Bell, he could see indecision in their eyes. They were taken back to their cells after neither asked for an attorney. Mike hand picked the guards who took responsibility for their well being.

Mike Stout was not new to the realities of the corruption that came with money and knew well that the real decision makers in this scheme would likely never see a court room or the charges they deserved. He also knew that his case could be easily swept under the rug simply by eliminating himself, Ichiro, and the evidence, just like the two assassins who had already been written off as a bad investment.

He knew that at some point as he climbed the ladder, a corrupt official in the FBI would likely squash their attempts to continue the investigation. Yet he also knew that thousands were dying now and millions would follow if they did nothing.

On the following Thursday morning Ichiro was called to his mother's side where he stayed and prayed until early afternoon when she passed into glory. He was numb, unable to focus, and disillusioned with the God to whom he had pledged his life. The age old question WHY weighed upon him like a stone. Why her, why now, why had God not healed her?

Haru sat by his son praying quietly while gently holding his wife's lifeless hand. He raised his eyes to his son and spoke. "Which of us shall not endure trials to find joy? Has she not found the joy she has always sought?"

Ichiro looked first at his father's haggard face, then at his mother's relaxed one that showed none of the rigors of the long battle she had fought, and nodded agreement.

~ ~

"Anson, you assured us that you had this matter well in hand and yet you continue to utilize incompetent labor that is unable to do their jobs. Now two of your finest are in custody, no doubt ready to spill their guts to save their worthless hides," the President's Chief of Staff shouted.

Anson, for all his bluster, was a fearful man, a man who believed in nothing but power and money and now he saw both slipping from his hands. When the phone went silent he began packing what few things he needed to travel out of the country. He had plenty of money stashed away and had made preparations for this moment all the while hoping it would never happen.

With a ticket in hand, his altered passport, and several thousands in cash he called for a taxi to take him to the airport. An hour later the taxi was found abandoned in the over flow parking at the airport with his corpse inside.

~ ~

Agent Stout had gone as far up the chain of command as he dared, he knew each man personally who was invited to the impromptu gathering but was unwilling to trust the upper echelon. He had quietly gotten a Judge to grant a search and seizure warrant and had confiscated several cases from different manufacturers of vaccines waiting for distribution to the elderly and had hidden them away at separate locations. Ichiro had verified the existence of the trigger introduced to the vaccines and had documented his findings in the event of his demise.

When word leaked out from several pharmacies that the FBI had confiscated the tainted vaccines, all hell broke loose with politicos and CEOs pointing fingers at one another. A last ditch attempt was made by the Attorney General's office to force the FBI to release the evidence, before they saw the handwriting on the wall and scurried to cover up their complicity in the matter.

Of course the White House circled the wagons and, knowing that the whole sorted affair would come to light, elected to break the news that THEY had discovered "tainted" vaccines and were moving hastily to take them off the market and prosecute the responsible parties. No indication that the introduction of such vaccines was planned and orchestrated by it would ever come to light.

Haru, like his wife and many others, succumbed to his illness two months later and went to meet his Savior with a smile on his lips. Ichiro has yet to find a cure, but has clinical trials underway for the vaccine that God may have prescribed to stop cancer before it starts.

The End

The End Game: An American

Prophecy

They waited outside the perimeter until the electro-magnetic air-burst had disabled all communications and transportation within a ten mile radius, before detonating the forty-four canisters inside the stadium. When they arrived, they came as mock SWAT teams in full battle dress, with gas masks and automatic weapons. No vehicle manufactured in the last twenty years had escaped the effects of the massive burst of radio waves which toasted their electrical components, thus eliminating any chance of pursuit.

The teams, their coaches, and entourages lay dead in their respective locker rooms, their lifeless eyes bulging from the effects of the gas. Soon afterward fans all over the stadium also crumpled and fell as the VX gas dissipated throughout the ventilation systems. The gas, being lighter than air, rose to the upper rim of the Sports Authority Stadium before being blown away by the light fall breeze where it became harmless as it dissipated into the atmosphere.

Most fans were lifeless when they arrived just after noon, but the few who were still breathing and throwing up putrid chemicals were quickly dispatched with automatic weapons fire. There was no resistance from security as they loaded carts with the day's gate receipts and quickly and efficiently rolled them to the waiting vehicles.

In the manner of street gangs, several took extra minutes to scrawl

"ISIS" on walls of opportunity as they passed, to prevent any from considering that it had just been a robbery rather than an attack on American soil. What could be more fitting than the great American pastime of football to be the world's stage for the first strike since 9/11?

Throughout the area, telephone conversations and television transmissions ceased without warning, although the source of the cessation remained unknown for several more hours. There was no sign of the intruders forty-five minutes later when the first of the law enforcement arrived at the stadium and reestablished contact with the outside world. Since the effected area had been at first unknown, no single area or cause was immediately suspect. It was 15:52 hours before the White House could track down the President who was recreating at Martha's Vineyard and finally convince him to declare a national state of emergency.

Reports were sent to every agency, the beat cops to the NSA were put on high alert without knowing who or what they were searching for. No evidence was left behind except shell casings that had been missed being picked up by the assailants. Those in leadership were quick to acknowledge the graffiti and point shaking fingers at those unknowns who had sworn death to the infidels.

Others took a more deliberate and reasoned approach, looking at all possibilities but keeping ISIS also at the top of their lists. When it was verified that the money had been stolen, that fact seemed to draw other suspects into the possible equation, thieves who might be using ISIS as a scapegoat.

~   ~

Don Strain was the senior agent at the FBI headquarters in Denver who had first responsibility to react to threats against the American government, both domestic and foreign. Don had just turned forty-six and now spent most of his time managing the "young lions" that were coming up through the ranks, from behind his desk or from his iPhone. He wasted no time regaining the hands-on leadership style that had earned him both his reputation and his current leadership role.

The death toll was still unknown but speculators spoke of numbers approaching eighty thousand, when they included both fans in the seats and those who worked behind the scenes to manage the stadium, provide security, maintenance, staff, players, and officials. The irony that Mile High Stadium had been the location where the pro-Islamic President had received the Democratic nomination in 2008 and had since shown himself sympathetic to their cause was not lost on his detractors.

Denver in particular, and the entire nation as well, was rocked to its core. Not since Pearl Harbor had an enemy struck so ruthlessly and so unexpectedly. The last was of course up for debate, many speculated that an attack, if not this particular one, was well known in the intelligence community and by the leadership who were either helpless or indifferent to preventing it.

Agent Strain spent much of the next six hours in communication with both his superiors and subordinates in addition to department heads from rival agencies, the Whitehouse staff, and finally the Vice-President. Ironically, the President had chosen to work through those in Washington who seemed to supply information which suited him and his press secretary rather than garnering factual, on the scene information. Strain saw on television, rather than finding out through the normal channels, that the President would be arriving the following day to assess the situation.

The few handfuls of survivors who had escaped both the lethal gas and the systematic slaughter which followed, had for the most part been those who escaped notice while traveling to or from their parked automobiles. Those forced to leave early for some reason or those arriving late and had gone unnoticed now considered themselves blessed by God. Witness accounts described the scene as macabre and otherworldly, like something out of a movie, the assailants dressed as uniformed police officers arrived and left in traditional black SWAT vans. Even as the shooting began, witnesses had at first suspected that there were other antagonists rather than the police. It was not until they watched some of their own group shot and killed that they realized the source of their peril and hid.

~   ~

When Penny picked up her phone she was relieved to hear her husband's voice, but as soon as he began to justify why he would not becoming home, all the years of tears and loneliness returned and her heart turned cold. She knew well that her rage was unrealistic, that there was an imaginable disaster in their city which had taken countless lives, that it was his job to pursue and arrest the perpetrators, and that she was selfish and demanding.

Perhaps it was those times in the early years when he could have let others handle the crisis but had chosen it over his family, or perhaps it was a menopausal thing, either way she did not care. She hung up the phone while he was still trying to rationalize it to her.

Strain was red faced and angry when he heard the dial tone, maybe they should have divorced rather than separating and attempting to reconcile, he thought. Maybe they had been wrong for each other right from the start. No, that was not true, he knew. They had been well matched, and he still felt love for her in spite of what had happened, it was losing their child that had driven the wedge between them.

She had never recovered, she still blamed God and him for taking

Lisa away from them. Was his faith stronger than hers he wondered, or was it that she had never really had it? Painfully, slowly, but steadily he had worked through the emptiness that had surrounded her death, by leaning on God and His words of comfort. Penny, on the other hand, had lashed out before withdrawing into herself. He tried to understand but could not. Tried to help, but failed. Eventually he quit trying and poured himself into his work.

"Hey Boss," Dimmick said, "where do you want me to start? I called everyone and told them to drop what they were doing and come in for a briefing."

Don smiled in spite of himself. Good old dependable Dimmick he thought, getting things done without having to be told, doing what needs to be done.

"Thanks Dim," Strain said. "I appreciate you getting' on top of it. I've been so bogged down with the brass I couldn't get off the phone to call you and ask."

"What do we know for sure?" Dimmick asked. "Do we have anything at all to work with?

Don shook his head slowly, and then answered quietly, "a few witnesses who identified the combatants as local SWAT and a few shell casings which may or may not lead us anywhere. They've identified the gas as VX, which has been on the black market for 20 years or more and last used in the Middle East a generation ago."

"Nothing that identifies them conclusively as ISIS, no eye witnesses who actually saw their faces?" Dimmick asked.

"Yes, no... well maybe," Strain answered. "Several were on the prescription drug Diazepam as a treatment for anxiety and it seems that it is an effective antidote for the gas. Problem is only the few who had the presence of mind to play dead were not shot and killed by the insurgents."

"We have sixteen in custody at a safe house who observed them without their masks," he added.

"And... ?"Dim asked smiling.

"And I don't know." Don answered. "For now no one except the team with them and you and I know they exist. I want to keep it that way until I know who we can trust."

"Does Washington know?" Dim persisted.

"No," Strain said flatly, "like I said, until we know who is behind this it doesn't get out of this office.

"Who is with them?" Don asked.

"Klaus and Baker," Dimmick answered.

"We're going to need two more teams that we can trust," Don said. "Do you think you can handle that?"

Don could see that Dim was already thinking about it.

"Should be guys without families or girlfriends to be calling and asking questions," he said thinking out loud, "but seasoned men who can keep their mouths shut."

Don nodded agreement. "When you get the names get back with me and we can go over it together," he said.

Strain took a call from the Governor and spent twenty minutes telling him what he wanted to hear without really saying anything. 'Maybe I should try politics' he said to himself after hanging up.

~ ~

It was 22:00 hours when JJ's arrived at the desk downstairs with Don's late lunch. As he sipped a Coke and magically made the footlong disappear, he began scribbling notes on a pad while scanning intel reports which were accumulating faster than he could read them.

Fifty-seven agents and twenty-two support staff were under his direct command, with thousands across the nation and around the world on electronic standby. He knew that teams, literally hundreds back in Washington, were evaluating thousands of messages and phone calls which had been placed and received over the past few weeks with a motive to find clues to the tragedy. He also knew that the turf wars between several agencies worked against, rather than with the FBI to gather information quickly. The NSA, CIA, and TSA were among those who wanted to be the one who provided answers to the White House and to receive the credit.

A hushed voice came over his personal line with a message that chilled Don's blood... "it's ours."

The call came from a friend in the lab who had been evaluating the gas in an attempt to narrow down its source and thereby the list of probable suspects.

"Keep it under your hat," Don said, "I'll meet you in five minutes."

Don went down nine floors and still made it in four. He pushed the button before using his key card and entered the lab. Bob was waiting for him with fear in his eyes and urgency on his face.

They took a private room, although none of the other lab rats were visible on the floor. "Kentucky," Bob said without hesitation, "the gas was markered as produced in the Kentucky facility in late 1959, should still be stored there according to our records."

Don's mind was in fifty places at once. "How do we find out who has had access?" he asked his friend.

Bob answered quickly, "I can have a list in five minutes for what it is worth, but with it being that long ago, who knows who or when it was stolen? It may have been gone for ten or twenty years and was re-placed with inert gas so no one would notice it was gone."

"Has there ever been a reported breach or break-in?" Don asked.

This time Bob smiled, "There is something in the personnel records just last year that looks suspicious in light of what we now know. A security guard was found dead of an apparent heart attack and his partner was summarily retired without pay shortly thereafter."

Don was following the scenario. "Does it say why he was let go?"

"No," Bob answered, "but the whole thing looks fishy because he never contested the firing or asked for settlement or retirement."

"Give me all the personal data you have on him," Don asked with conviction.

Bob rattled of the name, social, DOB, and last known address.

"My ears only," Don said, looking his friend directly in the eyes... "no one knows, and Bob, make several copies of everything and watch your back."

He left the lab and returned to his office, it was 01:27 when he settled into his chair and lit up the screen on his laptop.

~ ~

Deliberately Strain typed the name into the NCIS computer, and then erased it without hitting 'send'. He needed to know as much about the ex-guard as he could find out but found himself questioning the wisdom of using the company computer to do so. A nagging question didn't quite take form in the back of his head. His first year of training came back to him. When investigating, always question "who benefits the most from the crime?"

"Ben," he said into his personal cell, "this is Don, I wonder if you can do me a favor first thing in the morning when you get to the office. I'm thinking about selling my car to a guy and carrying the papers. I wonder if you could run a credit check for me."

He hit 'end' and sat the phone on the desk beside him. He knew he'd get some flack from his bowling buddy at the bank for even considering financing someone he did not know well. The old adage "if the bank wouldn't loan to him you certainly cannot afford to", was a wise one.

Sometime during the wee hours Don must have dropped off to sleep because he nearly fell out of his chair when his cell rang. It was 09:00 and many of the agents had already arrived and were catching up with each other around the coffee pot. Luckily Don had closed his blinds and locked his door before closing his eyes.

"Don, this is Ben," a cheery voice said. "What's this I hear about you going into competition with me?"

"Nothing like that," Don said, "just considering doing a guy a favor, they won't give me nothing as a trade-in at the lot and the guy needs wheels to get to his new job."

"Not supposed to do this," Ben said for the sake of his conscience, "but since you are such a good guy, why not."

Don gave him all the info he required then asked, "how long will it take? I promised to give him an answer today."

"Call you back in fifteen minutes," his friend promised before breaking the connection.

In less than ten the phone rang back. "You pullin' my leg or something ole buddy, this guy died a year ago somewhere down south," Ben replied.

"You sure?" Don asked, "Maybe you spelled the name wrong or maybe I copied the social down wrong."

"Or maybe," Ben said, "the guy is a con man and stole someone's identity. You're in the business, look him up yourself."

"Can't unless it's official business," Don lied, "they monitor every keystroke."

"Well, I'd steer clear of him if I were you, "Ben said. "See you Tuesday, you owe me a beer."

"Tuesday then," Don answered. "I'll buy you a pitcher!"

~   ~

A knock on the door followed by an attempt to enter drew away Don from his thoughts. He got up stiffly from his chair and unlocked the door and let Dim into the office.

"You look like hell," Dim volunteered, "musta spent the night here again. When you gonna learn?"

"Close the door," Don said quietly, "and sit down."

Dimmick did as he was told and looked his friend in the eye, "what's up Boss?"

"Can't talk here," Don said. "How about I buy us breakfast and go over the case?"

Dim smiled and replied, "maybe you should hit the shower first. Your hair's standing straight up and your breath would kill a horse."

Don made a face and flipped his friend the bird, then said, "Give me fifteen minutes and meet me downstairs. By the way, how about the relief team, have any luck?"

"Clark and Mason relieved them at 08:00." Dim said smugly, "they have orders to keep it under the radar. Did you hear about Bob down in the lab?"

"No, what?" Don answered, icy fingers encircling his heart.

"He was killed last night on his way home," Dim said, "Damn shame too, he was a good guy."

Don was having trouble breathing when he answered, "Fifteen minutes downstairs, not a word to anyone, K?"

What the hell, Don thought, as the hot water ran down his body, have I gotten myself into?

~   ~

"Boss says to rein your guy in," the voice on the secure phone said, "else he's likely to find himself in trouble he can't handle."

The Director wasn't used to taking orders from a no-name over the phone but knew well who the "Boss" was and what a long reach he had. Director Gerard picked up the direct line which connected the Washington office with the station in Denver, the phone rang four times before he broke the connection.

Strain was a good man, he thought to himself, as good as he had, and with his instincts it would not be easy to pull him off the scent without alerting him to the game which was already under way.

~ ~

"Penny, please pick up," Don said earnestly. "It's important." But the phone rang three more times before asking to leave a message.

In the lobby, Dim was flirting with one of the security at the metal detector while waiting for Don. Don smiled in spite of himself. She looked to be in her mid-thirties, dark skinned, athletic, and strong as an ox. Don would have bet a week's pay she could have whipped Dim on his best day without breaking a sweat.

"Where are you boys headed?" she asked deliberately accentuating her southern drawl. Jus' maybe I could git my boss to let me come 'long."

"Quick bite of breakfast before we go down into the dungeons and torture the prisoners," Don said, returning her smile.

When they got to the street, Don turned to his friend who was making for the parking garage, "let's walk," he said firmly.

"Assume we are under surveillance," he added, looking away from Dim's inquiring eyes. "Just listen and keep walking."

"Who...? Why...?" Dimmick began to ask.

"Don't know," came Don's reply, "but they've got long arms. Tell me what you know about Bob."

"Denver P.D. called early this morning as a courtesy after running the plates and finding it was one of ours. Apparently it was a hit and run," Dim continued. "They found a trash hauler a couple blocks away abandoned with damage to the front end. Poor Bob never knew what hit him they say, it took him broadside in the driver's door and his car burst into flames."

"Listen to me carefully," Don said seriously, while looking down at his feet, "something big is going on here and we are right in the middle of it."

"No shit, Sherlock," Dim replied. "We got 80,000 dead, invisible foreign jihadists on American soil, and we don't have a clue."

"Bigger," Don said, locking his eyes with his friend, "bigger than that."

The grin disappeared from Dim's face. "What could be bigger than that?" he asked.

Don changed the subject, "let's go have a visit with our witnesses," he said. "You grab a cab and I'll do the same."

Alarm clearly registered in Dim's eyes as he nodded and walked away from his friend.

When they arrived at the safe house, Denver's finest was there in full force accompanied by their Chief of Police and the Coroner.

"We responded to "shots fired" at 07:30 and arrived at 07:45 and found this," the Chief said, pointing to the carnage in the safe house. "No sign of the shooters or eye witnesses, just a description of a black sedan with four males dressed in SWAT uniforms," he added.

Clark and Mason each had been zippered before they could get off a shot, the fifteen witnesses had each taken two or three and had died where they had fallen.

The Chief looked Don in the eye and said, "Tell me about this."

"These were the survivors of the stadium massacre who we brought here for safe keeping," Don answered, shaking his head, "some good it did them."

The Chief shook his head, "maybe we could have lent a hand if you'd let us in on it," he said angrily.

"Or maybe you'd have lost some of your friends like we did," Don responded. "Whoever did this, they don't seem to care who they kill.

~ ~

The two agents rode a bus together on the way back to the office, as they traveled they talked.

"I thought you told me sixteen," Don said. "I only counted fifteen corpses."

"There were sixteen, but we had to take a woman to the hospital. She had an asthma attack and had trouble breathing." Dim said.

Both mouths dropped at the same time as they stood and pulled the cord to stop the bus. They grabbed a taxi and paid the driver an extra fifty to get them to Rocky Mountain Memorial stat. Ten minutes and three red lights later they were pulling into the emergency exit.

Dimmick stopped at the information desk and asked for the girl by name and was told no one by that name was registered. When she was asked to recheck, she asked if possibly she had been registered under another name. When they tried her initials, bingo, there she was third floor room 3012. Long waiting lines were in front of the elevators forcing them to take the stairs two at a time.

When they reached the third floor, both agents pulled their weapons, chambered a round and dropped their arms beside their leg at the ready before they opened the stairway door. The hallway showed no activity or traffic, the sign showed rooms 3025- 3051 to the left and rooms 3001-3024 to the right, they turned right. Their weapons were partially hidden behind their legs when they approached the nurse's station and asked directions. At the end of the long hall an orderly pushing a gurney looked over his shoulder and directly into their eyes.

The eye contact was sufficient for both to raise their guns and order the man to halt. He did not, in fact he reached under the covering on the gurney and pulled out a Russian-made AK. But before he could fire, both agents emptied their clips into him, dropping him instantly to the floor.

Amid screams from the nurses, Don flashed his badge and asked someone to call 911. In room 3012 a twenty-something woman sat round-eyed and shaking as they entered and identified themselves to her. Don had the presence of mind to call the D.P.D. Chief and request his presence at the hospital and a well-armed contingent of officers to provide security.

Out of courtesy, Strain waited for the Chief to arrive before questioning the woman. The entire interview was filmed and recorded on his iPhone before being transmitted back to FBI headquarters. What the woman had to say shocked both the Chief and Dimmick, but just verified what Don had suspected, the murderers had been white males who spoke fluent English and appeared to be American military types.

That his two agents had been "zippered" lent credence to the suspicion that they may have been Navy Seals or Army Rangers who were known to leave their signatures in the form of a zipper-like string of wounds up the bodies of their victims. Maybe mercs he thought, ex-military gone over to the other side.

~ ~

A small package was sitting on Don's desk when he returned to his office, inside a single 8GB thumb drive labeled in Bob's handwriting filled in many of the blanks of the puzzle. Sgt. Thom Silvers, the recently deceased security guard from the facility in Kentucky had been recruited from the ranks by the CIA and subsequently dropped out of sight until surfacing again as a guard at the Kentucky facility.

It was presumed that during the removal of the canisters the other guard became aware of the theft and had to be eliminated. But who had pulled his strings and who had taken possession of them, then waited a year to use the gas? Certainly not ISIS, Don reasoned, their coalition had not even been formed when plans for the use of the gas had been made.

Being careful to not leave a signature trace on his hard drive he took a clean thumb drive and copied Bob's information onto it, then slipped it into his pocket. He felt slightly foolish and somewhat paranoid at the suspicions that possibly he could not even trust everyone here in FBI headquarters, that the leak that had killed the witnesses and his two agents had come from within.

His thoughts were interrupted when his secretary rang his line, "Director Gerard is holding for you sir," she said.

"What the hell is going on there," Gerard shouted without pleasantries, "and how come I hear about the killing of our agents from an outside source?"

Caught off guard, Strain was slow to reply.

"Who were these fifteen civilians that you were holding incognito?" Gerard continued to rant.

Don supposed that someone within the Denver P.D. could have leaked the news, but wondered at how it had found its way so quickly to the Director if that were so.

He knew it would do no good to ask the source of the leak so he answered briefly. "Everything here is a mess and there hasn't been time to go over the details with everyone who thinks they should be copied in, with things moving so fast." He immediately regretted what he had said.

"You mean you haven't had time to include your Director in the events which have become the biggest thing since World War II?" Gerard asked sarcastically.

Don knew it would do no good to try and plead his case so he cut it short and apologized. "I am sorry, Director, I guess this thing has caught us all off guard and seems to be running ahead of the investigation with new events popping up every hour. Everyone from the Governor to the White House feels the need to be kept up-to-date and I have felt more like a PR man than an agent. I'll make it a priority to see that you are kept in the loop in the future," he said, trying to sound repentant.

"See that you do, Strain," Gerard said. "I've just gotten word from the White House that the President has chosen to postpone his visit until we can assure him that the situation is under control."

Don wondered now why he had been so quick to assume that the leak had come from within, why he had just assumed that this was some kind of plot rather than an attack is it had first seemed. He promised himself to try and distance himself and to move more slowly and carefully. He called Dim into his office.

"Dim, give me your take on all of this, tell me straight out what your instincts, as well as the facts, are telling you," he asked his friend.

Dimmick looked at him quizzically before smiling and beginning to speak. "I think that there is more to this than meets the eye," he began. "What that means, I am not yet sure."

Don waited without interrupting as Dim thoughtfully clarified what he was feeling.

"What is it that you are not telling me?" Dim asked turning the tables on his boss. "How does Bob's accident figure into it?"

Don had forgotten that his planned breakfast visit with Dim had been interrupted by the news of the shootings. He slid Bob's flash drive across the desk toward his friend. "I think this cost Bob his life. Take good care of it," he said.

Alarm registered on Dim's face as he accepted the offered storage device, stood and started to leave.

"For now don't download it, copy it, or leave any trace of it on your computer," Strain said earnestly. "Let's just keep it between you and I."

Dim nodded but did not answer.

~ ~

"Lab rat is toast," he said to the man on the other end of the secure line, "retrieved his memory stick and traded out the hard drive on his computer before torching the car. I think we have stopped the leak but this guy Strain is still nosing around, took out our guy before he could get to the last witness."

"Relax," Gerard said, "he's just doing his job and as long as we have not left any loose ends lying around, eventually he'll have to accept it for what it appears, a terrorist attack."

"I had a little heart to heart with him," Gerard added. "I don't think he'll be going off on his own again without telling me first."

~ ~

"Chief, this is Don Strain," Don said. "May I ask you a question off the record?"

The Chief was surprised by both the early morning call and the unusual request and answered the question with a question. "What's on your mind, Strain?"

"My boss knew all about the shooting yesterday even before I had a chance to call him," Don said. "Do you have any idea who may have been in a real hurry to report it to Washington?"

The Chief gave a little self-satisfied laugh before answering, "he caught you did he, playing close to the vest, not letting him know so he could take credit?"

"Wasn't me," he continued, "and I doubt any of my team knows the Director's number. The only one I told was the Governor."

OMG, Strain thought, the Governor had fingers in pockets all over Washington and it'd be just like him to call Gerard and try and "one up" him.

"Thanks Chief," he said. "I hope you don't feel the need to report our little conversation to him, do you?"

"Listen son," the Chief said in a fatherly tone, "I don't like secrets no matter who's keeping them, if you want me to keep yours you had better come clean with me right now and tell me what's going on."

"Lunch today, my treat, at noon at Carrabras on Tenth Street," Don said lightly. "See you then."

Don knew that he could not do this alone, he had to trust someone and up to now only he and Bob had known, but now Bob was dead. He dialed his home and was rewarded by Pam's recorder asking the caller to leave a message. He asked her again to call and hung up.

~ ~

Dim burst into Don's office just as he was picking up and getting ready for lunch with the Chief. He closed the door and turned toward his boss with both anger and concern written across his broad face.

"Does this mean what I think it means," he asked? Then not waiting for an answer, he continued. "Are you thinking this is an inside job, that someone other than the towel-heads pulled off?"

Don looked at his watch, it was 11:20 when he decided to let the

Chief wait if necessary.

"I don't have it all worked out yet," Don admitted, "but it is looking more and more like whoever did this thing has a motive even bigger than sticking a finger in Uncle Sam's eye."

"Who knows beside you and me," Dim asked, "how do you know who you can trust?"

Don just shook his head slowly.

"How about joining the Chief and me for lunch," Don asked smiling. "I still owe you for the breakfast we never had."

This time they took the company car but rode in silence, each of their minds was filled with questions needing answering. When they arrived, parked, and entered, the popular restaurant was nearly filled. The Chief was waiting for them at a booth in a corner near the back.

"Chief," you remember Dim from the scene yesterday," Don asked cordially. "I've asked Dim to join us and since I'm going to put both of your lives at risk, I thought I'd spring for lunch."

They looked at each other and then at Don. The waiter arrived with menus and made known the specials of the day and his personal recommendations before taking their drink orders and leaving.

"They tell me the veal is good," Don said, trying to keep the mood light.

"Get to it Strain," the Chief said harshly, "what the hell is going on?"

The waiter arrived just in time and took their orders.

Don spoke slowly and deliberately. "No one, I repeat, no one can know what I am about to share with you, can we agree on that?

Both men nodded after looking at each other.

"I am not sure of a motive yet," he said, "but here's what I suspect."

Both men listened without interrupting as Strain enumerated both what he knew and what he suspected.

The Chief spoke first. "What makes you think you can trust me to not run right to the Governor and spill my guts? Or... Dimmick here for that matter?"

Don started to answer but was interrupted as their meals were delivered to the table. The waiter refilled their drinks and bread basket before leaving again.

They ate quietly for several minutes before Don answered the Chief's question. "I can't afford to NOT trust someone, I need help big time and my instincts tell me neither of you can be bought nor scared off."

They accepted his dubious compliment and then started throwing out possible ways of proceeding. Don listened, commented, and then added, "my first priority is to find out where the leak is within my department."

"What I'm going to suggest," the Chief said, "could get you fired and maybe even jail time. If it were me, I'd work backward from your boss, get your hands on his phone records and start with who leaked the shooting to him, and then see where it goes from there."

"And, just how would I do that without tipping my hand?" Don asked. "I'd need to use our own resources and no one I know could pull it off without getting caught."

"There's nothing the CIA likes better than trying to find dirt on the FBI," the Chief laughed. "And, I just happen to know an ex-operative who has no love for Gerard."

"Black-ops guy?" Don asked.

"Something like that," the Chief said. "Let me visit with him a little without tipping our hand and see what he offers up."

~　~

"Don, this is Pam," she said and added, "I've moved out and in with my sister. I don't see any sense of pretending anymore that we are going to work this thing out. Your need to put your work first has always been the problem and you are never going to change."

Don was going to plead his case and try once again to explain what was expected of him, but stopped short and just said, "stay in touch and let me know if you need anything," before hanging up.

There he thought, it was finally over, maybe now he could put it behind him and move forward.

He had barely hung up when the phone rang back, it was Chief Brown. "We need to meet," he said, "how about a beer?"

At 19:20 Don entered Brewster's Pub on 42nd and was surprised to see Brown and Dim sitting like old friends in the back by the pool table, sharing a pitcher. He pulled out a chair and sat as Dim poured him a glass.

The Chief smiled boyishly and said, "I haven't had this much fun since I stopped getting carded."

They sat there, the three of them, in their Denver Broncos jerseys, like three middle-aged frat boys up to no good.

"He'd love to do it," Brown stated with a twinkle in his eye, referring to his unknown friend. "He says there's so much new techie stuff out that he hasn't used that it'd be fun just to try it all out."

"Are we going to meet him?" Don asked.

"Yup," the Chief answered. "Here he comes now with a fresh pitcher."

They looked up and into the pale blue eyes of the bartender who had a half-smile on his face. "This one's on me, gentlemen," he said, setting the pitcher on the table.

"Dim, Don, this is Bruno," the Chief said, inclining his head toward the fifty-something man standing over them.

Bruno was laughing when he replied, "Is it dim Don or Dim and

Don? Brownie makes you sound like a comedy act."

Don spoke slowly, "you know what we need, the Chief filled you in?"

"Sure 'nuff, it will be my great pleasure to take old pencil neck down if we can. I should have something for you before the end of the week," Bruno said as he returned to the bar.

~   ~

"The announcement is going to come a week from Thursday night," he said to Gerard. *"The President is going to flood the airways and announce the need for martial law until this crisis has been handled and the terrorists have been caught and punished. He's going to promise safety. He's going to invoke the war powers act and begin confiscation of non-registered guns. Homeland security is not constrained by the search and seizure laws. He's not waiting on Congress or for anyone to prove conclusively who is responsible. He's likely to also begin moving troops sympathetic to his cause into towns and neighborhoods with the promise to protect innocents as his platform. He has already retired nearly all of the capable senior officers in the military who could have moved against him. Congress will cry like a cut cat but too late to be effective, they'll stand impotent and disillusioned wondering how it all happened."*

Gerard replied, "Still, it seems a shame that so many had to die. Why do you suppose he chose Denver?"

"What better place than a liberal blue state that would be eager to embrace the government as the solution to their problems?" was the answer.

The Chief of Staff actually laughed into the phone before saying, "The Boss called them just "potting soil" in the garden he is planting, he told me that for this to work, citizens would have to fear something or someone more than they fear him."

"Does he really think they'll just hand him the country without a fight?" Gerard asked.

"If they need more urging he has already picked out a city as the site for a dirty bomb attack," the COS said. "Ever since they stopped believing in God they have been looking for a savior and he sees himself as a fitting replacement."

~ ~

Bruno had not only gotten the phone records for Gerard's home, cell, and office and had meticulously documented names and numbers from the call lists, but he had also fortuitously tapped his phones for new incoming calls. It was how he had brought the afore written account between Gerard and the President's Chief of Staff to the clandestine meeting on Friday, after the bar had closed.

"What do we do about it?" Don asked the group. "It is like a snowball rolling down hill."

"I doubt we can, if anyone on earth can," said the Chief sadly. "They are like sheep fleeing before a wolf, willing to jump off a cliff rather than turning to face him."

Bruno had invited himself to sit and figured himself now as a player. "What little common sense remains and who the public still has confidence in is the key to fighting this," he said. "We need to have someone credible to break this news who is believable, with a following, and who has no political leanings."

The room was silent as they absorbed what had just been said, then Dim spoke, "General Petrie and some of the top brass still have a loyal following, and guys like Colin Powell are well respected and apolitical," he suggested.

Don was actually smiling at his friend, "remind me to never underestimate you," he said. Then he added, "and from there the talking heads will spread the word if the liberal media will let them."

"But," Bruno reminded them, "we've got to move fast, to break the news before the President does on Thursday."

~ ~

"General, I'm calling you on a throwaway phone," Don began. "For reasons of national security I am asking you to trust me and return this call on a secure line."

Don and his small group sat waiting breathlessly for over an hour before the Wal-Mart prepay rang.

"How'd you get my private number?" the General asked gruffly, "and what is all this cloak and dagger stuff?"

Don took the lead. "I am with the FBI" he said slowly. "We have been investigating the tragedy in Denver, and have come across information I think you should hear. Are you willing to listen with an open mind to a recorded conversation between the President's COS and the FBI Director?"

There was no sound for what seemed an eternity, finally they heard the General exhale before he replied simply, "Yes."

The recording was played twice before being paused. Don resumed the phone and could almost hear the wheels turning in the officer's mind.

"You've got my attention," Petrie said, "but if this is some prank you better travel fast and far because I still have many friends who'd love to hunt you down and make sure you pay.

"Sir, I only wish it wasn't true," Don replied, "but it seems to be and I do not think we can afford to take the matter lightly We've reached out to you because we believe we can trust you and many like you who have been weeded out of the ranks, specifically for this reason. Will you try and gather as many as you trust and let me know where and when we may meet face to face?

"I'll call you back," came the terse reply. The line went dead.

The four men sat sipping their beers without speaking until the Chief finally broke the silence. "I'm a Christian," he declared to the group, "and a believer that the Word of God is true and correct. What I fear we are living through is what happens to a nation who turns away from God, as did Israel before being sent into captivity."

He continued, "we may have already gone past the point of returning to Him and are finding ourselves in the End of Times. If that is the case, there is nothing or no one who can stop the Evil One from establishing his reign on earth."

Three of the four gathered were born-again Christians, Bruno however, as a lifelong Catholic, seemed to be out of step with what the Chief had said. "So you are saying we just give up and wait for Christ's return, just stand by and not even try?" he asked.

Dim answered, "not at all, if that was the case we'd not have called Petrie or set plans in motion to oppose the President. I, at least, believe that God has specifically brought the four of us together in this place and at this time for His purpose, what that purpose is waits to be seen."

"I agree," Don concurred. "Each of us is uniquely positioned and I see it as no accident that we are here today."

The Chief nodded agreement.

~ ~

"Tom, this is John," the old general said pleasantly. "I've invited a few of the old guard to meet at the country club today for dinner and a visit, will you join us?"

Tom was Colonel Thomas Richards who had been Petrie's second in command in Afghanistan and a loyal man who had also been a victim of the administration's purge.

"Sure John," Tom answered. "Who all will be there?"

"Just a few of us old pensioners," Petrie said, deflecting the question in the event he was being recorded.

"We'll be looking for you about 6:00 then," he added before hanging up the phone.

On the desk in front of him were two lists, one with names of men whom he had or would trust his life to, a dozen including himself, the other... good men, but some of whom he'd not be willing to invite in until he was more certain of their allegiances. A Dirty Dozen, he thought to himself, remembering the movie from decades before and automatically casting himself as Lee Marvin.

He called Don's throwaway and reached him at his desk at work which lent credibility to his claim of the previous evening as being with the FBI. Don just listened.

The general was brief and to the point as he explained what had happened at his end. "I'll need to hear the recording again," he said, "so I can take notes to take with me tonight. At some point I'll also need a copy for them to hear in person once I've arranged a safe location."

"Done," Don said. "Let me know how, when, and where to send it." The connection broke and Don motioned Dim into his office where he shared the one sided conversation with him.

~ ~

"What did you get from the witness?" Gerard asked.

"Not much, I'm afraid," Don answered. "We seem to be at a dead end here. She claimed that they spoke English and looked Caucasian but nothing else of value. It makes me wonder if we have some ex-military ISIS sympathizers who have gone over and joined them."

Don knew that his boss was no fool and thus played it as close to factual as he could, leaving out of course his knowledge of the true reason for the attack.

"No way to trace the money, no fingerprints, no loose ends?" Gerard inquired.

"The money was gate receipts in the amount of about $1.3 mil, but no serials are ever taken at this kind of event. They appeared to have been wearing gloves," Don said truthfully, leaving out the detail that some shell casings may yet yield usable prints. "Of course, you already knew that the surveillance cameras were fried and of no use," he added.

"Well, keep at it," Gerard said. "I'm getting pressure from the top to get results."

He disconnected.

"No sir, Mr. Governor," the Chief said before repeating nearly word for word Don's speech, "we have nothing new but have our ears to the ground hoping someone will slip and say something to his girlfriend or to a snitch who'll give us a heads up."

~ ~

There were two large tables, each seating six, reserved for them in a private room at the local country club which catered to retired military. Most of those present had either served together or knew of each other by their achievements and as such held each other in high esteem. There was the usual ribbing and foolishness, cocktails, and war stories before the wait staff arrived to take their dinner orders.

When they had left, General Petrie stood and raised his glass in a toast to "America, the land of the free and home of the brave," watching carefully as each raised their glasses.

"Thank you all for coming on such short notice," he said. "I trust you'll enjoy my hospitality, rekindle friendships, and make new ones before the night is over. I have reserved a suite for us and a couple of decks of cards after we finishing eating. I expect to win my money back to pay for this before you go home," he added.

All four services were represented by careful design, Petrie knew that each leader represented a unique breed of American patriots. He and Tom of course were regular army, General Baines, who had commanded the Airborne Rangers, was seated across from a bird Colonel who had served under him, the Admiral and Vice Admiral were of course Navy, with two Captains, both submariners, a Brigadier had worked his way up through the Marine ranks and was flanked by two of his best Colonels, and a two-Star was still serving actively as a Pentagon liaison to the Air Force and was expected to move to the Joint Chiefs, if not forced out before.

"So, John," Baines said as their dinners were served, "when are you going to tell us why we are really here?"

Petrie tried to look hurt when he answered, "Isn't just being with old friends enough reason, Bob?"

His response brought a round of laughter from the assembly. One of the navy captains mumbled something about Amway or a pyramid scheme under his breath, but loud enough for all to hear.

They finished their dinner and pushed back, several ordering a dessert and an after-dinner drink. Some of them used the occasion to have a cigar and inquire about the wives and children of their friends.

"Well men," John said standing, "time to grab your checkbooks and follow me upstairs to the waiting tables."

The eleven, some still in their late forties and others nearly seventy, but all having given their lives to the defense of their country, followed behind their host obligingly.

~   ~

There were three round tables, with two decks on a table waiting as the men filed into the luxurious suite. There was a stocked bar and a tray of snack foods beside it.

John took several minutes to introduce each man and go quickly over their careers before asking that they seat themselves with others whom they had not served.

"Before we begin," Petrie said, "I'd like to have a commitment from each of you that what goes on in this room goes no farther." He looked each man in the eye and held their gaze until the expected nod came.

His "Wal-Mart special" rang appropriately and he answered the call before putting it on speaker mode. He sat the phone on the table, as the room grew quiet and he introduced the two conversationalists.

"The announcement is going to come a week from Thursday night," he said to Gerard. *"The President is going to flood the airways and announce the need for martial law until this crisis has been handled and the terrorists have been caught and punished. He's going to promise safety. He's going to invoke the war powers act and begin confiscation of non-registered guns. Homeland security is not constrained by the search and seizure laws. He's not waiting on Congress or for anyone to prove conclusively who is responsible. He's likely to also begin moving troops sympathetic to his cause into towns and neighborhoods with the promise to protect innocents as his platform. He has already retired nearly all of the capable senior officers in the military who could have moved against him. Congress will cry like a cut cat but too late to be effective, they'll stand impotent and disillusioned wondering how it all happened."*

Gerard replied, "Still, it seems a shame that so many had to die. Why do you suppose he chose Denver?"

"What better place than a liberal blue state that would be eager to embrace the government as the solution to their problems?" was the answer.

The Chief of Staff actually laughed into the phone before saying,

"The Boss called them just "potting soil" in the garden he is planting, he told me that for this to work, citizens would have to fear something or someone more than they fear him."

"Does he really think they'll just hand him the country without a fight?" Gerard asked.

"If they need more urging he has already picked out a city as the site for a dirty bomb attack," the COS said. "Ever since they stopped believing in God they have been looking for a savior and he sees himself as a fitting replacement."

You could hear hearts beating within their chests but little more except their breathing as John hung up the phone. He looked back into the eyes of the capable men who had just promised their secrecy and noted eyes filled with both fear and anger.

It was General Baines who spoke first, "that son-of-a-bitch, he thinks he's God does he, I'm here to tell you he is not."

Petrie let them vent for several minutes before he called them to order. "What are we going to do about it?" he challenged them. "The men who brought this to me see us as the nation's best last hope. And," he continued, "as you have just heard, our time is short."

"What do you propose?" the Admiral asked John. "You've had longer to think this through, share your ideas with us."

"First," John said, speaking slowly and carefully, "we must consider that we may already be too late, there may not be a way to galvanize the nation against him, and second, those who are still active duty will be committing treason which is punishable by death."

Several of the younger men present looked at each other but said nothing.

Tom took the cue. "I'm very junior here but I do not see us as having much of a choice, we pledged our allegiance to the flag and not to the man. True that he is supposed to be the Commander-in-Chief but I personally feel no allegiance to a man who would kill Americans for his personal gain."

Every head nodded in agreement.

For the next hour each man had his say, each proposing ideas which were then discussed and either accepted or rejected as a group. When it came down to the final plan, each participant was to carefully choose his own dirty dozen whom he felt he could trust and verbally share what he had heard while swearing each to secrecy.

Only the twelve in this room would know all of the players, those down line from them would only know the name of the man above him who had recruited him. Each recruit would be empowered to follow his own conscience and his allegiance to the nation as opposed to the regular chain of command to which he would most certainly find himself at odds.

In addition, each of the original twelve would have the responsibility to orchestrate a circumstance which would give him the widest possible audience when they each broke the news to the nation at the same time. It was expected that there was a possibility of a leak when the circle got beyond the first generation, therefore the down line was to be unaware of both the time and date of the revelation.

~ ~

Back in Denver, Don had received the fingerprint results from the shell casings. Three separate sets were identified as ex-military, all of which were shown as having been killed in action. Ghosts, spooks, originally probably CIA but now gone rogue, the fifty or so men who had invaded the stadium now answered to a new and merciless master. Using their duty assignments Don was able, by association, to determine other likely deceased soldiers now working covertly in the

United States against the interest of the country.

Photographs of the suspected terrorists were given to the Chief with instructions to show them only as persons of interest in ongoing investigations, without specifically naming which investigation.

~ ~

The Wally phone rang and Don took it to the rest room with him, where he was filled in on that the decision had been made to break the news first thing on Wednesday morning, thus scooping the POTUS by twenty four hours. They feared if it broke earlier the opposition would have time to regroup and possibly retaliate. Don approved and shared it with his three compatriots.

Monday morning, as things were coming down to the wire, two of the many suspects were picked up by the local police and then whisked away as material witnesses to an unknown holding area to be questioned. Dim and two hand-chosen agents interviewed them at length with instructions to get information at all costs. Both had been well trained and neither supplied useful information.

"Coming out," a term often used in other circles, was the one the 'Dozen' used to refer to their pending announcements. Each had carefully planned their own coming out with a nationally known television host who had no idea of the topic of conversation but was pleased to have such notables as their guests. Each of the twelve carried with them two copies of the recorded telephone conversation, presumably to be played to a national audience.

~ ~

"We are in position," the COS said to Gerard, "we are right on target, I spoke with the President last night and everything is a go. We have a sizeable military force in every major city awaiting his instruction to impose martial law. He expects little resistance."

~   ~

Author's first note: Contrary to my instincts as an author and with several possible endings floating around in my head, I have chosen to not second guess whether the American public would see this as an occasion to return to God and put their confidence in Him or through fear put their trust in man. It is my hope that we never need to come this close before finding that any man is a poor substitute for God.

~   ~

Author's second note: After giving some thought to it, I've decided for the sake of my readers that I should pen an end to this little story. I've chosen to write the ending which I hope would happen but still have a nagging fear that no mention of our nation in the Book of Revelation is significant, and we should not be so arrogant as to believe our well-deserved fall will not happen... whether now or later.

~   ~

Wednesday morning on the east coast began like many others, with the exception of the several morning shows welcoming well known and powerful guests from the four branches of the military. Not fifteen minutes into the interviews, various television stations and indeed their network affiliates were scrambling to find suitable solutions to the "coming out."

Less than ten minutes later they began to receive significant pressure from Capital Hill but too late to stop the "shout that was heard around the world," as many came to call it. Social media sent it worldwide in minutes, touching everyone who had network connections. Military bases were told to discontinue access to television and computers but had no way to stop individual access, which quickly was rebroadcast among the men in the ranks.

The rank and file on the streets was either wildly supportive or looking for criminal charges for every member of the current administration. Clergy could hardly remain neutral given the statements which so clearly and openly blasphemed God.

Reminiscent of the 9/11 tragedy, churches both with and without affiliation were filled with the repentant and prayerful alike. Our loving God, so long suffering as He watched His children turn from Him, chose this point in history to empower the Holy Spirit to touch mankind as never before, softening hearts and opening ears and eyes of both the unbelieving world and those who believed but had walked away.

The revival that many had prayed for all of their lives encircled the world in six days, touching even the remotest parts. The seventh day ushered in the promised rapture, with one third of the world's population leaving the mortal world to become part of the immortal and everlasting kingdom of God.

The End

– DANisms –

- If you tell the whole truth, you are bound to offend someone. If you tell a half truth, you will offend everyone.

- The drumbeat of our hearts marks not only the passing of time, but also the moments until eternity.

- The tensile strength of love cannot be measured.

- You'll never fly unless you try, and never fail unless you quit trying.

- If you have a friend that you cannot buy, cajole, or intimidate; value him because he was sent to help keep you from taking yourself too seriously.

- If you look at today as just an extension of yesterday, you will completely miss its uniqueness and grow weary and bored.

- As you try to analyze your life and judge your worth, remember not everyone is Moses, someone had to take down and put up the Tabernacle and... presumably someone else wove the fabric for the robe that Jesus wore.

- Sometimes when we feel the need to shine, we try to do so by dimming the lights around us.

- There is much I'd do differently if I had the brains to know what it was.

- As young Christians who struggle to find our place in the world, it may help to remember that our place is not in this world.

- If you don't seem to "fit in", sometimes it is because you don't "fit in", which is not always a bad thing.

- You are living yesterday's choices. If you desire that tomorrow will be different you must choose to make it so today.

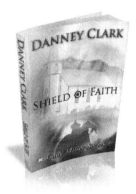

SHIELD OF FAITH

"One more thing, Red, then if you want I'll shoot you, okay? Thing is, if you should beat me, I go to Heaven to be with the Lord, but if I beat you, where do you suppose you'll go for all eternity? Have you thought about how long forever in Hell might be?"

Red cursed again. "You don't worry about me miner, you worry about your little family here after I shoot you!"

SHIELD OF HONOR

Amid the explosions and aerial displays that marked our nation's Independence Day, he heard a yell followed by a louder and sharper report that was closely followed by a second and third. Cady, in his blue uniform with Kevlar vest and duty belt, was lifted off his feet by the impact and fell fifteen feet from the pier into the East River.

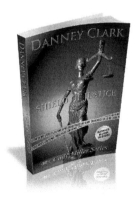

SHIELD OF JUSTICE

Unknown to others, Cady Miller was a dangerous man, having the physical and technical abilities to inflict mortal injury. His lean stature and rapidly advancing age belied his physical prowess. His pale blue eyes now retained their 20/20 vision by the use of contacts lenses, but more importantly he used that vision to see things others often missed. Skills honed through years of training and discipline allowed him to maintain an edge others frequently lost as the years caught up with them.

These and other offerings available at the Author's website:

www.danneyclark.com / www.danscribepublications.com

– AVAILABLE NOW –

Chronicles of the
WIDESPOT CAFÉ

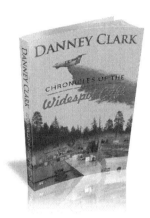

After college, nine years went by quickly, I moved from job to job, town to town, never having a close relationship or a feeling of belonging. I worked in every industry, every position, in every field garnering small success but feeling alone and empty inside.

To my credit, I lived on my earnings, not touching my investments, but spending all that I made. I drove taxi, waited tables, painted houses, sold shoes, installed computers, cooked, drove truck, did construction, or whatever came along.

Young, healthy, and able to learn quickly, I was easily employable. I have never owned a house, a car, or been married. Like King Solomon, I searched for the meaning of life, and like him, I didn't find it. I had many friends, none close, no ties, few responsibilities, felt no kinship to anyone except possibly the friend and partner I knew in college. But he had now moved on and marched to a different beat.

Then one day I stopped by the Widespot Café intending to just have a meal... that day, it all changed for me. I met Mae and Jib.

SPOONFULS FROM
HEAVEN

This little book is much the same as a savory stew, made up of both large and small bites of various ingredients and with a dash of this here and a pinch of that there added for flavor.

Some readers will enjoy the texture and the flavor of the whole stew, while others may enjoy one ingredient more than another.

Eaten as a meal, it is my prayer that you will find it both filling and satisfying.

These and other offerings available at the Author's website:

www.danneyclark.com / www.danscribepublications.com

– AVAILABLE NOW –

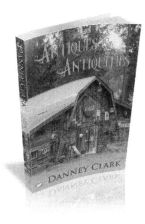

Antiques & Antiquities

Often we do not understand the importance of things (and people) that come and go in our lives.

Seldom do we take the time to evaluate their God-given purpose, nor question why we have been brought into contact with one another.

Perhaps we should....

– About the Author –

Danney Clark is first a practicing Christian, then a husband of nearly 50 years, a father of two daughters, and grandfather of two granddaughters. He is also an Idaho native who values and enjoys the outdoors in all of its varied forms that are so apparent in Idaho.

When he finds a challenge, he is passionate about pursuing it with diligence before moving onward to the next. Questionably an accomplished cook, he devotes much of his time to serving the homeless community and his church home.

His passion for many years has been writing and most recently, God-inspired Christian fiction, or "adventure with a spiritual message" as he calls it. He sees life as an adventure to be enjoyed, appreciated, and shared. Recent retirement has encouraged him to do so.

Made in the USA
San Bernardino, CA
21 June 2015